𝓑

𝓊37

THE
NEW
ART
OF
FLOWER
DESIGN

THE NEW ART OF FLOWER DESIGN

Deryck Healey

Villard Books   New York   1986

Copyright © 1986 by Marshall Editions Limited

All rights reserved under International and Pan-American Copyright Convention. Published in the United States by Villard Books, a division of Random House, Inc., New York, and simultaneously in Canada by Random House of Canada Limited, Toronto. First published in Great Britain by William Collins Sons & Co. Ltd.

Conceived, edited and designed by Marshall Editions Limited 170 Piccadilly, London W1V 9DD

ART DIRECTOR   John Bigg
ART EDITOR   John Meek
TEXT EDITORS   Vivien Armstrong
                        Carole Devaney
PICTURE COORDINATOR Zilda Tandy
MANAGING EDITOR   Ruth Binney
RESEARCH   Jazz Wilson
PRODUCTION   Barry Baker
                        Janice Storr

Library of Congress Cataloging-in-Publication Data

Healey, Deryck.
   The new art of flower design.

   Includes index.
   1. Flower arrangement. I. Title.
SB449.H43 1986   745.92   85-40724

ISBN 0-394-54675-X

Typeset by Tradespools Ltd, Frome, UK
Origination by Reprocolor Llovet SA, Barcelona, Spain
Printed and bound in West Germany by Mohndruck Graphische Betriebe GMBH

9 8 7 6 5 4 3 2
First American Edition

Contents

6   Introduction
8   The Classical Influence
10   The Oriental Influence
12   The Nineteenth-Century Influence
14   Collecting Ideas

16   *Colour and Flowers*
18   Tones and hues

20   *Lighting*
22   Up, down and around
24   The play of light

26   *Hallways*
28   Landings and stairwells
30   A welcoming table
32   Designer graphics
34   Making walls work

36   *Dining Rooms*
38   Unexpected containers
40   Mini collections
42   Modular designs
44   Visual balance
46   Contrast and harmony
48   A changing focus
50   Uninhibited arrangements

52   *Food and Flowers*
54   Dining in style
56   Tempting trays
58   Vegetables and desserts
60   Salad days

62   *Living Rooms*
64   The floral screen
66   Creating visual links
68   Decorative harmony
70   Unabashed graphics
72   Looking-glass themes
74   Curls, swirls and twists
76   Repeating movements
78   Exotic collections
80   Interpreting a theme
82   Baroque elegance

84   *Shelving*
86   Two by two
88   Shelves galore
90   Flowers at the window
92   Above eye-level

94   *Bedrooms*
96   Bedside surprises
98   Get well soon

100 *Bathrooms*
102 Mirror images
104 Reflective themes

106 *Kitchens*
108 A brighter breakfast

110 *The Big Day*
112 Pastoral romance
114 A bridal pathway
116 Festive mantelpieces
118 Christmas flowers
120 Party tables

122 *The Office*
124 Working flowers

126 *Dried Flowers*
128 Scaled to size

130 *Making the most of flowers*
132 Choosing flowers
133 Flowers on the move
134 Flower care
136 Choosing containers
139 Working mechanics
141 Techniques of floral design
144 Drying and preserving
147 How to light flowers
149 Using colour
152 Favourite flowers

156 Glossary
158 Index
160 Acknowledgments

Introduction

Flowers give life and freshness to a room. Add a few blooms, place them where they will catch the early morning sunshine or the glow of soft lamplight, and a room immediately takes on an air of life and conviviality. There is no need to make stiff or elaborate arrangements, or to follow a set of rigid rules. Relax, enjoy using plant material and let your imagination have free rein, taking care beyond the "florist bunch-to-vase" mentality.

The New Art of Flower Design is a guide to making individual arrangements that match both your mood of the moment and the season of the year. It shows how to get the most out of flowers by handling them sympathetically—playing with them even—so that they work like coloured pieces of a jigsaw puzzle, slotting into place within each arrangement and within the room setting you select.

Creating new flower designs can be as simple or as complex as you choose to make it. The arrangements that were made for this book vary in scale. There are minimalist arrangements, using single blooms, and extravagant floral "fantasies," intended for special occasions such as weddings. Between these extremes is a huge range of shape and form, including highly sculptured effects, surreal new flower "species" made by using foliage and flowers from different plants, and the exotic combination of wild and cultivated material.

In every flower design, the elements of light and colour are vital to both the contrast and the harmony of the finished effect. Colour comes, of course, from the plant material itself, but also from the arrangement's container and the roomscape in which it is placed. Learning to use colour in flower arrangements as an artist uses his palette is critical to the making of a design statement. Light—direct and reflected, natural or artificial—has much to do with the final effect of an arrangement and can be manipulated, if artificial, to change an arrangement's emphasis. A stark twiggy design, strongly uplit, creates a gladelike pattern of shadows in a room, for example, while a strong downlight makes the design the room's focal point.

Flower design is an intensely practical and enjoyable activity, so to make the information in these pages as accessible and as useful as possible, the book takes you on a room-by-room tour of the home, showing how each has unique design needs, and how a design or colour theme can be carried through the whole interior scene. In the hallway, for example, flowers should say "welcome," while in the living room they should interact with the colours, textures and mood of your decorations and possessions. In the dining room, flowers can act not only as elements in a design but also as a bond between the guests at your table. The mirrored and other reflective surfaces of the bathroom are ideal for creating amusing visual effects with flowers and foliage. Flowers in the kitchen, especially if they are those of herbs to be used in cooking, can be both practical and decorative at the same time. The ideas are infinite—all you need to do is to dream them up with the help this book provides.

Take your inspiration for flower designs from everything plant-related that you see around you, whether exotic or everyday. Picture postcards, photographs of flowers and gardens, wallpaper, fabrics and china designs are all good sources. So, too, are museums and galleries, which show how past masters have interpreted flower designs in still-life paintings.

With the help of many friends and colleagues, and especially Graeme Roberts, I have had enormous pleasure in creating this book. I hope you will have just as much fun creating your own flower designs.

Deryck Healey

To my mother, Irene Healey: to Betty Roberts; and to Aunty Ve Hulett who has shared with us from childhood one of the most beautiful gardens.

The Classical Influence

In Greek and Roman times, the love of flowers and flower arranging was as strong as it is today. Only a few of these masterpieces remain, in the form of mosaics and some wall paintings, but countless Greek bowls, vases and urns are decorated with swags and garlands.

No comparable flower arrangements were produced after these great works until the Renaissance. Then, in Italy, Luca della Robbia (*c* 1399–1482) discovered a method of applying brilliant enameled glazes to terra-cotta. He made decorative plaques showing white fruit and flowers modeled to form garlands surrounding gentle Madonnas. The distinctive white glaze on a soft blue background is still a design influence today.

Glowing studies of flowers appeared in illuminated manuscripts, in herbals and florilegiums, and even in paintings by masters such as Albrecht Dürer. But the flowers were usually treated only decoratively, as part of the background, or symbolically. Flower paintings as such were not recognized as works of art until the late sixteenth century when there was a resurgence of interest in all plants, stimulated by the hundreds of new types being brought back to Europe by explorers. Dutch and Flemish artists translated the excitement at these exotic wonders—tulips and fritillarias from Turkey feature in many a canvas—into some of the most magnificently robust flowerpieces of all time.

Flowers, fruit, food and wine in silver containers were placed on tables covered in richly patterned carpets. The vases, full to overflowing, were flanked by butterflies, snails, birds' nests and eggs. Colours were brilliant and bold, the light seeming to radiate from the flowers themselves. Paintings were usually done over a period of time, so within one picture you would see spring, summer and autumn flowers side by side; in one painting by Jan Breughel, there are more than 25 varieties.

In the eighteenth century, tastes changed and in France, the colouring and design of Sèvres porcelain brought in a fashion for pale pastel flowers. Madame de Pompadour, mistress of Louis XIV, the Sun King, even decorated her châteaus with delicate porcelain flowers.

The Oriental Influence

The word "oriental" is used to describe both Chinese and Japanese cultures. But in the art of flower arranging, there is a clear distinction between the two.

The Chinese are devoted to flowers for their intrinsic qualities. Their arrangements owe little to so-called design and much to the perfection of beautiful blossoms, to intense or subtle colour, and to fragrance. Attention is given to decorative containers and flowers are often set in vases of rich imperial yellow.

It is the Japanese culture that has had the strongest influence in the West. Schools and clubs can be found in most countries that teach the art of *ikebana*, which means "beautiful flower arrangement." The Japanese tradition of *ikebana* is the skillful creation of graceful line and harmonious proportion, with an underlying emphasis on the interpretation of nature through symbolism. Oriental manuscripts, paintings and porcelain are a rich source of reference.

Ikebana is a living art form in which the artist develops an individual style using all types of flowers, foliage and containers. Free-form objects, such as stones or pieces of wood, sculpture, and modern materials, including metal wires, are all incorporated. Flowers are imbued with new life and meaning by subtle and careful groupings to create a mood. With only a few blooms, quiet and repose can be expressed or an occasion celebrated; joy and peace can be brought to a home. This quality of goodwill is part of the Japanese philosophy of life. An arrangement is made with the object of bringing pleasure to family and friends and, on special occasions, to convey a silent compliment to an honoured guest.

To give an oriental touch to your own flower arrangements, you must make strong use of space, proportion and scale. The concept to bear in mind is that "less is more." Create centers of interest with flower heads—an uneven number is preferred— and display the structure of the plant to show its special characteristics. No flower should be used out of season and, most importantly, the elements of the design must be combined with skill to convey an individual style, a mood or an inner feeling.

The Nineteenth-Century Influence

The true master of flower painting in the nineteenth century was Henri Fantin-Latour. One of his friends said of him, "Fantin studied each flower, each petal . . . as if it were a human face . . .," and certainly his work shows the great pleasure he derived from the most common of country and garden flowers, especially roses. He paints his flowers in free relaxed bunches and mixes species and colours in a beautiful patchwork of texture and pattern: a glass bowl of pansies or a large drinking glass of soft pastels, pinkish-white and buttercup-yellow roses one can almost smell, their stems cut short and the full blooms bunched into a posy. The patterned oriental vases and clear glass containers he used are still a popular choice for flowers today.

Toward the middle of the century, artistic styles began to change greatly. The flower study became more intimate and informal, even domestic, often as a result of the new art of photography. The camera recorded details of interiors, table arrangements, gardens and plants as they were at a particular instant. This sense of immediacy influenced the approach of painters, as did the theories of the growing school of Impressionism. No longer was there a wish to reproduce every petal or leaf in loving detail; colour and light, and the colour of light, were all that mattered. Observe, for example, the way Manet captures the magic and colour of flowers in his paintings.

Freed from the conventions of earlier times, many great artists have since given an insight into original ways of looking at flowers. Van Gogh, famous for his sunflowers in a tall pottery vase, painted many other equally good flower studies, all with a strong earthy richness. In this century, Raoul Dufy painted flowers in ample light-hearted arrangements. And Matisse exhibited his striking mastery of colour by his bold use of the technique of pattern on pattern, setting his bouquets against Moroccan table coverings, rugs and wallpapers.

Today, flower painting seems to have gone out of fashion, but the use of flowers in domestic decoration has become popular, with textile and wallpaper manufacturers producing a vast assortment of designs. More than ever, people are linking floral arrangements to their way of living— borrowing from the artists of all periods to create their own twentieth-century style.

Collecting Ideas

Inspiration for flower designs can come from many sources. Most art galleries have works by great flower painters and it is rewarding to look at these and learn from them. Seek out paintings by Fantin-Latour to appreciate his casual elegance. The bold strokes of a Matisse canvas show how to use colour confidently, while Dufy's spontaneity demonstrates how to free your own arrangements. The rich earthy tones of Van Gogh and the bright green roses of Chagall show an exuberant awareness of nature and the effect of light on colour, which the painters are offering to share.

Few can hope to own such masterpieces, but you can make a collection of poster or postcard reproductions to use as visual references and to help spark your imagination. Do not limit your collecting to these, however; often a close-up of a mosaic or embroidery, or a page of an illuminated manuscript will germinate an idea. Snap up anything, however loosely connected with flower art—pictures in newspapers and magazines, for example, even an unusual combination of colours in an advertisement for cosmetics or food will do.

Of course, everyone has their favourite pictures and mementos of travel or vacations: Delicate seashells, a brilliant silk scarf, a piece of pottery. Riffling through a miscellaneous collection of such treasures can trigger your imagination and be the first step toward the creation of new flower designs.

The inward eye is stimulated to extend the boundaries of flower décor to create a mood or atmosphere by the recollection of huge bouquets in places such as the Metropolitan Museum in New York, Christmas decorations in famous department stores or such travel images as temple flower tokens presented by pilgrims in Sri Lanka.

Each person finds inspiration in a variety of different things. By using these visual reminders as a starting point, give free rein to your creativity and the "art of flower design" will take on a new dimension.

EXAMPLES FROM THE AUTHOR'S huge eclectic "inspiration collection" include: Postcard reproductions of flower paintings by artists, traditional and modern—Matisse, Chagall, Fantin-Latour, van der Goes, Cézanne, Picasso, Gaugin, Arcimboldo's 16th-century portrait and Tessa Traeger's 20th-century photographic portrait.

Vacation snapshots, a surrealistic collage by Bill Brandt, a Victorian postcard with "Nellie" spelled out in forget-me-nots, colourful advertisements for foods torn from magazines, a flower tribute on a Los Angeles car radiator. The collection grows continually, almost on a daily basis.

Colour and Flowers

Colours in nature are infinite, a fact most clearly demonstrated by flowers. Not only do colours vary from plant to plant of the same species and variety, but from flower to flower on the same bush, and even within each petal. A seedman's catalog may describe a flower as pink or red, but words beggar description, for the colours may range from palest almond-blossom to deep rose, magenta and a velvety red that is almost black.

The impression made on the eye by a flower's colour depends on several factors. First is its character, whether it is warm or cool; second, its brilliance or transparency; and third, its texture. Light, too, can affect colour. For example, artificial light causes yellow to lose intensity, pink to gain depth and blue to recede.

THE SECONDARY COLOURS are made by mixing together two of the primary colours in varying proportions. Blue and yellow produce hundreds of greens, from the sharp lime green of spring leaves to the almost blue needles of some conifers. Yellow and red give oranges that range from sunny apricot to fiery autumn tints. Red and blue create all the purples and mauves.

Green is the colour most restful to the eye; it is the colour of nature and of rebirth in the spring. Orange, even more than yellow, is uncompromisingly positive: the deeper the tone, the brighter the colour. Purple is not abundant in nature; most of its manifestations are in flowers—the deep royal-purple of irises, the intense blue of gentians, the blue-purple of violets and lavender, and the soft mauves of lilac blossom.

RED, YELLOW AND BLUE are regarded as the three primary colours; that is, the colours that, as pigments, cannot be produced by mixing the other two colours together. They are the pure bright colours that carry a simple direct message when used in flower arrangements. Yellow is linked with sunshine and is the colour to use to brighten a dark corner or cheer up a gloomy day. Red is the colour of vitality and energy. Strong and bold, it demands attention, particularly in combination with nature's neutral, green, which is red's exact opposite. In the same way that a distant landscape appears blue, blue flowers tend to blend into the shadows, giving an air of tranquillity and coolness.

TINTS AND SHADES. Large areas of pure colour, without gradation, are seldom seen in nature. The most brilliant red tulip, when you study it closely, has petals that exhibit both tints and shades of the colour. Tints are those hues which, in pigments, result from adding white to the pure colour; shades are produced when black is added. In flowers, the tints are the pastels: Creamy yellows, smoky blues, delicate pinks and hazy mauves, all of which blend harmoniously. The darker hues—intense blues, magenta, carmine pinks and deep crimsons— are the shades. The most successful flower arrangements are often those in which carefully related colour types are used together.

17

Tones and Hues

WHITE FLOWERS are often thought to be the quintessence of "chic" or style. Certainly, white on any scale—tall white lilies or miniscule stars of gypsophila—brings light into a room.

White looks freshest backed by clear greens, a combination found naturally in many types of variegated foliage. And green flowers, such as molucella and some euphorbias, can add an unexpected note.

A green and white, tone-on-tone arrangement almost makes itself, but bunching and grouping flower types gives definition. Add interest by the skillful use of contrasting textures, scale and shapes, such as the pebbles on the vase that repeat the rounded flower shapes.

JEWEL-BRIGHT COLOURS of similar intensity shine out of a bed of rich green, the colours seeming to glow against the contrasting background. Red, the exact opposite of green, would leap out of the arrangement, but this almost shocking pink, although it throbs with vibrancy, remains a part of the overall design.

The purple of the iris is tonally closer to the dark green, and although not as cool as blue would be, it still tends to recede slightly. But the contrasting stripes of yellow pollen on the petals enliven the purple, so it plays a forceful part in the design. Touches of white lift the whole arrangement.

This mixture of deep colours is visually exciting in a way not possible with tone-on-tone schemes, such as green and white.

A RICH MULTI-COLOURED DESIGN is produced by mixing colours of the same tonal value. Rather like a bag of confetti, the whole blends, with no single colour really standing out. Do not be afraid to mix colours; look at the multitude of colours in the flowers of a herbaceous border. There are contrasts, sometimes subtle and sometimes bizarre, but nature never clashes. Similar tonal values will always work in a flower arrangement.

FASCINATION FOR THE EXOTIC, for the sheer exuberance of sunny tropical colours of an intensity not previously seen outside the greenhouse, is easy to indulge today. The lacquer reds, flashing oranges and brilliant pinks are all available as foliage, cut from potted plants. Crotons, for example, display a great variety of coloured patterns in their leaves.

This splashy array of rich dark foliage is set in a Chinese vase, with a speckled blue pattern, against a neutral background. The glossy gay colours are echoed in the marble tabletop, the oil painting and the shiny bowls.

Lighting

An indispensable part of flower design is good effective lighting, whether the flowers are lit by natural light streaming in through a window or door, or by artificial light directed on them with spots from the sides, above or below.

Light can dramatize, shift the emphasis, change the scale and form, make playful shadows and silhouettes on the walls and ceiling—in fact, lighting can transform the whole mood of a room, bringing life to its furniture, objects and plants.

Modern lighting and lighting techniques have opened up many new ways of displaying flower arrangements. Pin-point lighting gives a strong emphasis; sidelighting and dimmer switches make for soft shadowy effects; uplighting creates a dramatic theatrical note; downlighting bathes a design in a pool of focus. Colour too can be affected—made to sing out brightly or rest quietly in muted tones to echo subtleties of the room.

MORNING SUNSHINE lights up a cool dark hallway where large bowls of daffodils are set at floor level in a pool of natural light. Knowing your rooms and where the sunlight will fall is a great advantage when placing your arrangements.

LIGHTING flowers that are naturally dramatic serves to emphasize further their sculptural shapes and texture. Six glossy anthuriums, set in florist's foam covered with moss, present a theatrical spectacle, with one huge heart-shaped leaf giving the design an off-balance effect.

Up, Down and Around

DOWNLIGHTING from a ceiling spot rests on a mixed arrangement, providing a focal point in a library with subdued lighting. The flowers are freely arranged at varying heights; stems, usually seen as dark lines, glow against the dim background as if in a photographic negative. Short-stemmed flowers lie close to the rim of the basket and delicate sprays of foliage are placed at random to create a soft pattern of shapes.

The light picks out part of the pattern on the container and embraces the small basket alongside, where dried rosebuds nestle. The dark wood table is enveloped in a pool of light and shadows play across its surface. Like a small oasis in a sea of books and Eastern carpets, it invites you to sit down and read awhile.

Wild flowers and grasses are perfect for such a display, their graphic qualities enhanced by downlighting or a spotlight which throws their shadows against the wall.

By experimenting, you will learn to match the lighting and flowers to the mood you wish to create and discover more of the intrinsic qualities of the plant material used.

NATURAL LIGHT shines through this big bundle of daffodils, loosely arranged in a clay pot, glazed on the inside only. To protect the surface of the seventeenth-century oak refectory table, a circle of plastic was cut to the size of the base and placed under the pot. Set against a backdrop of water, willow and sky, with a glimpse of daffodils growing beyond the lake, this sunlit arrangement appears totally uncontrived.

UPLIGHTING is an exciting and relatively new decorator technique which can significantly change the mood of a room and the objects in it.

An uplighter placed under a glass console table creates an almost surreal effect, with the top of the arrangement seeming to float in the darkness beyond. The whole form of the display changes from what it was during the day—new shapes appear, the stems are highlighted through the glass vase, colour is heightened and shaded from light to dark, more detail is evident in the brightly lit areas.

Uplighting is also effective with potted plants. A bird-of-paradise plant or a large palm, lit in this way, throws fantastic shadows on the walls and ceiling, quite out of proportion to the size of the plant itself. Experiment with the lighting to create special theatrical effects, which are especially fun at party time.

Low-voltage bulbs do not overheat or harm plants. Coloured bulbs give an interesting monochrome effect. A wonderland of colour can be created by fixing branches that have been painted white in a large metal bucket and shining different coloured uplighters on them from all sides.

The Play of Light

MIRRORS AND UPLIGHTERS combine to produce a fabulous display of pussy willow atop a bedroom fireplace. The Italian glass urn of classical proportions is transformed into the trunk of a tree whose branches glow with tiny points of light. A tracery of fine lines and curves is cast on the walls and ceiling, the image doubled in the mirrored backdrop.

Moving the uplighters sideways, backward or at more of an angle changes the scale and clarity of the shadows. Even a small arrangement can be transformed into a giant by experimenting with the placement of uplighters.

Artificial light can be manipulated to change and emphasize the shape of an arrangement. In the same way, natural light can be exploited to underline the special qualities of flowers. By placing an arrangement where it will catch the morning sun or be silhouetted against the evening sky, the flowers are seen afresh, in a different light to create a whole new picture.

THE TRANSIENT NATURE of light can be observed at close quarters as you laze around on a sunny day, watching the light play over a flower arrangement in the conservatory. A bunch of flowers is tightly tied with raffia to hold the stems erect in a glass flask. The scene changes again and again as the light moves across the petals and table, visibly altering relationships, colours and shapes. For a few brief moments, the water and pebbles sparkle, then one by one the gerbera heads are lit, while a spot of yellow pollen on an iris petal may be illuminated next. The focus is constantly shifting with the hours, recreating the design in a pattern of changing emphasis.

Hallways

The hall is the introduction to the home and the atmosphere of welcome should be apparent as soon as you cross the threshold. The hall is therefore an important area, to be regarded as another room, and although you do not usually linger there, a warm reception is immediately created by having flowers decorate the space, whether as fresh or dried arrangements.

The constant passage of people through the hallway is an opportunity to experiment with bigger, bolder and more unusual flower designs. There is often space for taller arrangements, standing on the floor or in a stairwell. A hall table offers a place for flower arrangements on any scale, even miniature posies in individual containers. A country cottage or city apartment, often unoccupied for long periods, becomes hospitable at once when dried grasses or flowers are there to greet you on arrival.

Open your hall door and you are outdoors, thus the hall is a natural extension of the garden. Projecting this feeling inside is refreshing; translate the essence of the season in your flower designs. The theme set in the hallway can be continued into the other rooms in your home.

A MIXED BOUQUET of summer flowers and massed leaves with exotic proteas is an essential part of the tablescape. More flowers placed in a child's sand bucket add to this eclectic scene, backed by a *trompe l'œil* painting linking the real and illusory in a collection of unusual objects.

STAIRCASE LANDINGS can be brightened up with flowers. A bunch of sunny tulips placed on a shelf makes a welcome beginning to the day. Long stems are allowed to flow in natural graceful lines. Shorter-stemmed tulips with a few gerbera tucked in form a soft crescent arrangement.

Landings and Stairwells

RANDOMLY ARRANGED garden flowers are a joy to behold. Their effect can easily be spoiled by overelaborate display; the gift of a perfect country bouquet assembled by chance has a simple charm.

Freshly picked flowers placed haphazardly in a bucket of water for an overnight drink stand on the cool tiled floor of a stairwell. Each time a nearby door opens, perfume wafts through the house and the roses, daisies, wild grasses and alchemilla catch the morning sun in an explosion of colour.

A GLASS UMBRELLA-STAND enhances the graceful lines of wild holly branches which, stripped of leaves, are seen to perfection and magnified through the water-filled container. By placing this tall arrangement on a half-landing, the design catches the eye as you ascend the stairs and again from above as you pass by.

Sprays of holly provide festive decoration at Christmas time, but after two weeks the glossy leaves become brittle and begin to fall. Stripping off the leaves creates a fresh look instantly, with the scarlet berries thrown into dramatic focus and the dark stems accentuated against a white background.

LARGE DESIGNS can be accommodated in hallways and their height made proportional to the rise of the staircase. Bare branches make particularly dramatic displays and have the advantage of not obstructing the sunlight sifting through the house.

The pussy willow branch is like an indoor tree and provides a surprise welcome. In the daytime, sunlight catches the pale furry buds in a joyful celebration of winter's end and at night, dramatic

shadows are thrown on the wall when the hall is lit. The design is positioned to make a delicate frame for the sculptured bust on its tall pedestal.

Use a branch of pussy willow in need of pruning and cut it into suitable lengths before the first buds open. Sprays of pussy willow give 6 to 8 weeks pleasure in the house and even longer in dried arrangements.

A metal Christmas-tree stand is useful in arranging a large branch. It has a bonded container with cross screws for supporting the branch in water and is heavy enough to remain perfectly stable, even when holding a considerable weight. Here the stand has been placed inside a Greek rush basket and moss conceals the mechanics.

A Welcoming Table

MIRRORS are useful in a dark hallway to reflect the light, and sometimes a view of the garden, into the interior.

Here a trio of miniature stylized topiary trees is reflected in squares of mirror glass, both behind and below. The effect is to multiply the arrangements, creating a continuous vista of flowers and foliage.

To make such "trees," line 3-inch clay pots with strong plastic, each wedged with a cone of damp florist's foam rising about 2 inches above the rim. Starting at the top, insert short cuttings of box (*Buxus suffruticosa*) into the cone to cover the foam; this can be done up to a week in advance of your final design. At the last moment, summer cornflowers

and daisies are nestled among the box leaves, making a hybrid tree of mixed flowers and foliage.

A WORKING HALLWAY is a repository for all sorts of bric-a-brac such as umbrellas, coats, shoes, letters and a variety of other personal things. The hall table can become a display area for small treasures, art objects, shells and mementos, all of which can be changed or rearranged for continuing interest. Play about with the placement of objects, balancing the colour and shape of large pieces such as

lamps or pictures on the wall; smaller items can echo texture to form a fascinating tablescape into which your flowers are incorporated.

A bowl of foliage looks and lasts well on a hall table. By contrasting a variety of textures and shapes, you will have a leafy arrangement that holds interest for weeks. Soft-coloured sprays of foliage, such as the silver-grey, coin-shaped leaves of young eucalyptus, allow you to add a few bright flowers for a special touch.

Designer Graphics

SIMPLE DESIGN, elaborate flower—strelitzias, the aptly named birds of paradise, are among the most spectacular of flowers and are seen at their best in an unfussy arrangement, dramatically silhouetted against a plain background. The single stems can be arranged into an unruly chorus line, with angular heads pointing inquisitively in all directions.

DANCERS on a Burmese lacquer box accompany the flowing lines of the strelitzias, which take on the appearance of figures frozen in a floral movement. Just three exotic blooms can set the imagination working. Play with the lighting and all sorts of interpretations can be contrived, as if you were making pictures from the flames of a fire.

WITH HEADS HELD HIGH, strelitzias are regal flowers and were named for the wife of England's George III, Charlotte Sophia of Mecklenburg-Strelitz, who was a patron of botany. The heavy flowers and long stems call for firm support and Frascati wine bottles make good containers for single arrangements.

Strelitzias are wonderful value and last for several weeks. But even when they are past their best, the flowers and great paddle-shaped leaves make interesting additions to dried winter arrangements.

Making Walls Work

A WALL BRACKET may be the only space where you can put flowers in a narrow hallway. But placed on a sunny wall near the front door, a flower "mobile" is created with delicate foliage swaying in the breeze.

A rococo *chinoiserie*, this gilt wall bracket shows a mandarin holding up an umbrella that forms a shelf from which willow and orchids hang, quivering in every current of air. Tall grasses and long sword-shaped lily leaves would also look well in such an arrangement.

The flowers and foliage are held securely in foam set in a plastic tray wired to the bracket and camouflaged with a trim of ivy leaves.

CANE BASKETS set on a paneled wall complement these earthy arrangements of dried flowers and seed pods, twisted ivy stems and pheasants' feathers. Dried material is ideal for small arrangements in a hallway. It needs little care and can easily be added to or replaced. To perk up a display or change its mood, add a fresh flower in a vial of water.

Another advantage of dried material is its light weight since no water is needed. Baskets can be attached to the wall with florist's fixative and the flowers arranged in dry foam on the spot.

Feathers are useful accessories in dried arrangements. With their beautiful markings, they blend naturally with dried material and polished wood; they can usually be acquired from game or poultry suppliers.

AN ORCHID-SHAPED white china wall vase displays a random collection of flowers and leaves gathered from the garden. This is an informal "add-to and take-away" arrangement, a new flower placed as a faded one is removed. Water is checked every day and the container washed thoroughly once a week for a new beginning.

Wall vases were very popular earlier this century and fine examples in Art Deco styles can still be found. They were made in a variety of shapes—cones, shells, classical half-urns, masks and heads. Basket holders designed for hanging plants on patio walls are adaptable, attractive and lightweight for indoors, but they need inner plastic containers if fresh material is to be used.

Dining Rooms

Whether you are eating simply with family or friends, entertaining guests in a grander style or dining alone, the dining room should never be without flowers. Flowers on the table create a mood of conviviality and sense of occasion or, to the lonely, can give a much-needed "lift." Even when the dining room is empty of activity, flowers still have a place in its everyday décor. At any meal, the table is a bond between diners, and flowers have a part in forging that bond. Your choice of plant material and containers helps create a total effect.

Seating guests around the table automatically brings them into an involvement with the flowers and the shape of your arrangement will dictate the relationship of each diner with the flowers. Thus with arrangements of different shapes, diners may feel themselves to be above, below or even within an arrangement, although flowers should never be so tall as to obstruct conversation. Avoid strongly perfumed flowers that "compete" with food.

A LANDSCAPE IN MINIATURE is created at the table in a roughly woven willow basket. Thus the freshness of the garden is brought inside a conservatory. Individual blooms appear to be growing from a mossy carpet. The first spring flowers are chosen to delight guests: Tiny plants such as violets, miniature ferns and primroses, either in their own flower pots or with the moist roots wrapped in plastic wrap secured by rubber bands.

Individual blooms may also be placed in water-filled jars hidden in the soft green moss. For practicality, the basket is lined with watertight plastic.

A CENTERPIECE OF FLOWERS in a basket complements the oak and brass setting of a weekend in the country. The garden atmosphere is captured in pale lilac, set with jewel-bright anemones flowing from an oblong basket. The same mix of pastels and accent colours could be created with other combinations of floral textures and hues, using spiraea, gypsophila or wild carrot in place of lilac.

The basket has an inner container wedged with moss; the flowers are loosely arranged in floral foam to form a sweetly scented haze.

Unexpected Containers

THE "FLOWERING FRUIT" is a surreal and unexpected dining table decoration. Here, the gleaming half-cored apple complete with daisy is an amusing alternative to an individual place setting or specimen vase. The natural sheen of the polished fruit creates a subtle contrast with the man-made lacquer of the tray.

The apples can be placed directly on the table, grouped as a centerpiece on a contrasting tray or used to decorate a cheeseboard. Other fruits or vegetables can be similarly adapted as containers. Pumpkins and melons are large enough to accommodate a plastic inner container for a buffet table arrangement. Fruit hollowed out for use in this way may need to be shaped at the base for stability, with other small fruits piled around and linked together with cocktail sticks to prevent them rolling away.

A SQUARE GLASS ASHTRAY filled with floating daisies can act as a centerpiece when surrounded with individual "flowering fruits." The use of the flower heads alone creates a polka-dot pattern, with additional flowers providing flair and a dash of colour.

IMPROVISATION ENHANCES a party mood. Underlining the welcome is a light-hearted arrangement which lifts the atmosphere of the meal.

Unusual containers are fun to use. On this occasion, a brand-new cookie sheet lends sparkle and humour to what would otherwise be a formal black and white Wedgwood table setting. Choosing perfect blooms, cut short, float a single flower head in every space. Select each for its intrinsic beauty and bring their varying shapes and colours into focus.

This witty design can be made with the same species of flower in varying shades or in a contrasting checkerboard of colour. The flowers float in pools of water and the candlelight reflects in the drops scattered on the tray.

Another improvisation with kitchen equipment is the use of metal pudding molds as candle holders, the candles wedged in firmly with moss.

Metal molds as individual mini-arrangements can also be a part of each place setting. These can be identical, or personalized for each guest to indicate a seating plan, with or without name cards.

Guests immediately feel at ease in an atmosphere of spontaneity. Gifts of flowers are not always easy to arrange on the spur of the moment, but appreciation is warmly evident if the giver sees a few blooms immediately tucked into arrangements already placed about the house, the main bouquet gift left in water for later attention.

Even if fresh flowers are not available a bowl of shiny apples, an array of nuts arranged on a wooden platter with a few dried flowers, or a glass cake stand piled with grapes or lemons is welcoming. Your "landscape" need not be centrally placed; it can be to one side or in a corner, to give the table a livelier, more personal look.

Mini Collections

LIQUEUR GLASSES on an ovenproof glass dish are set on a lacquer tray which acts as a showcase for a display of flowers and berries. Individual arrangements allow scope for drawing attention to buds and attractively veined leaves. Select the first buds of spring, precious exotic blooms or simple wild flowers whose subtlety can often be overlooked—all can be brought to the table to be seen in close-up, displayed as jewels for your guests' delight.

Groups of miniature vases set out on a salver or dish can be removed during the main course to return with the coffee tray when space is available.

IDENTICAL SPECIMEN VASES set on a wine coaster form the basis of a more formal tablescape. With birdlike angularity, the irises rise from the silver circlet. The arrangement of the flowers, with heads poised in every direction, enables guests to view their wild spiky outlines from all angles.

Choose both buds and fully open flowers to emphasize dramatic silhouettes.

Flickering candlelight adds a feeling of movement to the interplay of stems refracted in the water. A sequence of spot lighting further emphasizes the theatricality of the formal décor. Create the design so that stem lengths and water levels vary.

MEDICINE BOTTLES (*left and opposite*), each featuring a single bloom, make a fascinating table setting. They invite guests to handle the flowers, smell them or move arrangements about, thus participating in the enjoyment of the flowers without upsetting the design.

The sinewy stems, arranged in a collection of medicine bottles of semi-opaque greenish glass, seem to dance along the line of vision. Notice that in this choreographed design the stem lengths vary, the flowers at different levels to give a range of colour accents. The stalks form a delicate screen which invites personal involvement; the flowers are seen from all around and may even appear to come face to face with their viewers.

The colour of the bottles is repeated in the paper fan that forms the oriental background to this balletic design. The light glances through the fan, through the glass and between the flower stems. On the handwoven striped table runner, the porcelain's stark simplicity is a contrast in style. Crafted raffia tumbler holders blend with the earthy colours of the napkins.

Acquire small bottles and liqueur glasses to use as individual containers so that such an arrangement can be made to "grow" according to the number of guests sharing the table or as your mood becomes more expansive.

Modular Designs

THE REPEATING MODULE is always visually exciting. It can be created with flowers as well as with other objects. Permutations of repeating floral units offer endless variation, either in formal central groupings or informal casual arrangements. They can be placed in lines or in squares, circles or triangles.

The roundness of spherical modules is emphasized by the judicious use of plant material. Peony flowers form bold rosettes of colour framed by dark green peony leaves. The single lily leaf breaks the circle like an exclamation mark.

THE SHAPE IS SOFTENED by the addition of sprigs of *Alchemilla mollis*. Like its partner on the left, this design creates an entirely new "species" of flower—an exotic mutation with a surreal quality.

EACH MODULE may incorporate different species of flower in toning colours or identical blooms in blocks of pure colour. Extend the theme illustrated opposite in tones of cerise and mauve through to pastel pink. The shape and texture of each flower is especially important in single-colour designs. Here spiky chrysanthemums contrast with the smooth spheres of tulips and again with the shaggy domes of double chrysan-themums. Play about with the plant material, appreciating that the special qualities of each flower add interest to colour modules; the boldness of the colour squares seen from above is like an English Tudor knot garden.

To create such a module, cut the flower stalks to a uniform length and insert the flowers in a geometric pattern, starting at the corner of the square container. Place the flower heads in rows of four to six along each side, then fill in toward the center in a regular sequence. The container should be fitted with cubes of wet floral foam wrapped in moss and secured with raffia.

LILIES ARE GROUPED in the same container, but on this occasion the flowing petals cascade over and around the bowl forming a giant "single" flower. The structure of the speckled petals and jaunty stamens lends itself to a less formal design which can nevertheless be used as a repeating unit of the module scheme.

Visual Balance

DIFFERENT TYPES of plant material, used in visual balance to maximize their intrinsic qualities, evoke a feeling of lightness and harmony.

The strong, broad upward thrust of spear-shaped iris leaves gives strength and shape while the reeds add a crisp linear quality. The severity of the line is softened by the fluttering leafy silhouette. The diagonal movement of the two sculptural containers is repeated in architectural planes, with the contrasting foliage acting as a kind of plumage to add an element of surprise. The daffodil buds are the only changing element in this design. The nature of the balance they lend to the whole changes with their vase-life; as they open, they alter that balance dramatically.

THE GRAPHIC STRENGTH of the blue mirror painting by Roy Lichtenstein is reflected in the deep blue of the Bristol glassware and jug. The muted tone of the tablecloth reinforces the blue and white theme, underlining the decorative motif. The bold outlines are softened by the airy bouquet of daffodils, ferns, freesias and double daffodils linking the middle distance. One single cerise carnation provides the jaunty focal point which draws attention from the wall to the table and back again.

To express a freshness in informal arrangements, loosely bunch the flowers in the hand, place them directly in the jug, then lift the material so that it falls back into a relaxed position.

Contrast and Harmony

NATURAL COLOURED BAMBOO contrasted against a dark background of patterned textile shows off the wild roses in a dramatic modern design. The containers are made from a bamboo cane cut into sections of various lengths and then bundled together with string. Cut each bamboo section below a notch; water can be poured in and will be retained by the natural partition at notch level. But to be sure there will be no leaks, place single flowers in glass vials of water and slip these into the bamboo containers. You can improvise by using a "vial" made of tinfoil filled with water and wrapped around the stems. The bamboo sections can be put together in various ways to make different designs or they can be used as individual containers.

ROMANTIC PASTEL SHADES of sweet peas and roses blend with a background of floral wallpaper. A garden atmosphere is created by placing the roses in a willow basket "nest," linked with the bird design on the jug and the

roses theme painted on the Victorian dessert plates. An oriental touch is added by the paper lantern and bamboo cluster container. The various elements combine to form a romantic still-life arrangement.

Inspiration for such a design, combining flowers and fruit, comes in part from the romantic realist paintings of the Pre-Raphaelite artists Dante Gabriel Rossetti and William Holman Hunt. The oriental touches are inspired by Whistler, who was greatly influenced by Japanese art.

It is rewarding to study the work of such great artists and the earlier flower painters of the Dutch and Flemish schools. They will spark your imagination and inspire you to extend your flower designs.

But do not follow their arrangements slavishly; use them to develop your own style and intuitive sense of colour, form and texture.

A Changing Focus

As the Focus of a meal changes, so you can introduce new design elements. The exotic and the unexpected can come together, for example, as unusual textural combinations.

Mixing fresh and dried flowers, leaves and fruit, and blending them against a cane-patterned ikat cloth (*left*) stresses the oriental mood, carried through in the selection of bamboo steamers as containers. Bold waves of movement are formed by the giant dried bamboo leaves, which swirl out of the succulent fruits. The bamboo whisk creates a stiff artificial flower form, while the dried anthurium, saved from a previous arrangement, has a softening effect.

The sprays of fragile orchids, placed in a glass vial of water, are slipped obliquely into the design and bring it to life. Their asymmetrical shaft of sunshine freshens an otherwise muted arrangement. The sculptural qualities of the fortune cookies add further interest.

The fruits, cut and ready for eating, create new forms as surprising as the arrangements whose table they share. Each is augmented with an individual orchid blossom.

A footnote: Never discard fresh material at its final stage. This arrangement illustrates how pale shades of dried flowers and leaves have an affinity with understated colour schemes and extend the use of your flowers.

THE AFRICAN DISH (*above right*) laden with a harvest of fruit appears to float like a water bird. The deep green ivy leaves are like the wing feathers along the bird's side. Individual flower stems tucked into such a design are kept fresh in their own small water containers, such as the glass vials sold with orchids. Moist florist's foam sealed in plastic can also be used, the leaves and stems inserted through the plastic and the fruit nestled between them.

An Unfolding Arrangement with a hedgerow quality was created at the beginning of a country weekend party in spring. An assortment of flowers and foliage, new leaves and twigs was tucked into an antique tureen placed on a china platter. Guests and their host witnessed, over the following days, the enchantment of new leaves and buds unfolding. A horse-chestnut twig picked at its "sticky bud" stage gradually disclosed its fuzzy new leaves, while buds of scented daffodils, auricula and primroses opened to bring a breath of spring into the house. An empty bird's nest added a textural contrast in keeping with the design's concept.

Uninhibited Arrangements

HOMEMADE CONTAINERS and simple posies make perfect gifts from children, who can be introduced to the joy of flowers by being encouraged to arrange them in their own special way.

The delight of spring flowers shines through in the use of glass jars decorated with enamel paints by children. In the two arrangements above, a treasury of wild and cultivated material is loosely put together. The secret of this delicate touch is to place flowers intuitively, with affection for each bud and leaf.

The third crownlike arrangement is made up of rings of grape hyacinths (*Muscari*) and tiny pinks topped by a single red tulip.

Such simple jars of flowers are easily portable and it is fulfilling for children to make their own bouquets which can be taken to the bedroom at the end of the day.

On a practical note, remember that immature spring foliage may wilt unless it is conditioned really well. Total immersion in a bath of tepid water overnight is usually sufficient; but to avoid disappointment when using sprays of foliage which have just broken into leaf, it is wise to place the stem ends in boiling water for half a minute as described in the practical section on p. 134.

EMPTY PLASTIC BOTTLES make amusing, and practical, containers and come in a huge range of colours and shapes. Throw inhibition to the winds when you use such fun containers: Experiment with colour combinations and use flowers lightheartedly with flair and humour. In this design, the reeds and grasses have been employed as a visual link that draws the eye across the four vivid containers, which form a harmony of shapes and colours.

Whether you choose the vibrant primaries used for packaging bleach and detergents, or the pastel shades favoured for shampoo and make-up, ensure that plastic containers are thoroughly washed before you use them.

Plastics, being unbreakable, are ideal for parties and can be stippled or sprayed with paint or glitter. For bigger arrangements simply cut off narrow bottle necks with a sharp knife or scalpel. If the arrangement is in danger of being top heavy, add pebbles inside to weight the container.

Food and Flowers

The presentation of food allows tremendous scope for the imaginative flower designer. Leaves, flowers, petals and fruit can all be used to transform a plain plate of food into a glamorous and appetizing dish, fit for a king and queen. Food should give pleasure to the palette and to the eye; it should stimulate the appetite and the imagination and be not only mouthwatering but also eye-catching. Consider the presentation of oriental food, the delicacy of Chinese and Japanese dishes or the exotic foods of India and Malaysia; for centuries, food has been decorated to offer a visual delight to the partakers. In fact, in many parts of the world, food—whether classical French cuisine, rich Caribbean dishes or ethnic foods from Africa and Mexico—is presented as a work of art. Mealtimes are treated as a celebration of the joy of living and joining with family and friends in a pleasurable activity.

The art of the table has been practiced by Renaissance princes and wealthy Europeans for centuries, right up to the present day. Art museums are places of inspiration, with some of the finest examples of table décor painted by the Dutch Masters, showing food and fruit in various stages of preparation and decoration. Although the boar's head, a ceremonial dish garnished with a bright red apple in its jaws, is hardly the normal fare of a twentieth-century homemaker, it does serve to spark the imagination to adapt ideas from history and art.

When decorating food, choose material that is appropriate to the flavour and texture of the dish in hand. Remember, too, that you need not spend hours on intricate and complicated designs; the simple ones are usually the most effective.

TRANSFORM A FRUIT into a flower for a surprise attraction at the end of a meal. A summer melon takes on the appearance of a giant exotic bloom. Neatly sliced and fanned out from a center of elderflower sprays, the melon is given a mock stem and leafy branches to form a table centerpiece on its pale moon of marble.

To decorate a buffet side table, separate canned fruits into colour units and place them in glass cylinders of varying diameters and heights. Such a display can be prepared well in advance and rewards you with an exciting decorative scheme of contrasting colours, textures and forms. Consider, for example, columns of orange slices, pears, red and black berries, green figs, pineapple rings and melon balls.

Fresh fruit finger food can be treated with the same imagination; glazed fruits also look wonderful in simple arrangements or piled high in pyramids. Table napkins, plates and fingerbowls add the final coordinated touch.

Dining in style

SKEWERS TOPPED with fresh flower heads (*left*) add a delightful touch to an after-dinner surprise of sweet ripe melon, scooped out in a boat shape with bite-size pieces piled inside. This is an easy-serving idea that can be used with all sorts of soft fruits.

To make, remove the stem from the flower and pierce it with the sharp end of a skewer or cocktail stick. Long-lasting flowers, such as daisies, single chrysanthemums or carnations, are best in warm weather; keep the flower skewers in a cool room until needed.

COMBINING FISH AND FLOWERS does not readily spring to mind (*below left*), but such decorative presentations can be surprisingly successful. The pink flesh of the salmon trout, with small flower heads laid along its side, looks attractive on a bed of fresh vine leaves. A swirl of baby asparagus adds the finishing touch.

THE JAPANESE believe in the total integration of food, garnishes, presentation and surroundings. Demonstrated by an inspired choice of simple and beautiful objects to hold appropriate food, the colour, texture and arrangement of a meal create a visual feast. The essence of its beauty is ephemeral—the same food, garnishes or occasion do not occur twice.

The traditional black lacquer tray (*right*) shows the food to great effect. Three slices of salmon are arranged beside a carrot-centered lemon bouquet, the stem fashioned from cut and curled cucumber.

The presentation of today's *nouvelle cuisine* can be said to be influenced by the Eastern style: Food, flowers and leaves are displayed to make a tempting pattern of colour, texture and shape.

Tempting Trays

ENHANCE THE VISUAL IMPACT of the lunchtime meal by linking the soft colouring of the food and the table decoration. Puréed vegetables surround a terrine in which asparagus spears and half-moon carrot slices are revealed as flower patterns when the terrine is sliced.

The more relaxed you are at preparing and presenting food, the greater will be your enjoyment. Develop an attitude toward the serving of food that reflects your personality and style of life. Experiment with new methods, glean ideas from restaurants and trips abroad. The table is a conversation opportunity to be exploited in amusing and surprising ways; look out for books about famous hosts and hostesses, dazzle family and friends with your *joie de vivre* and bring a spirit of enthusiasm to everyday meals.

Using unusual containers to create a special mood in a table setting is fun. Cane, willow or china baskets make good containers for imaginative groupings of flowers and food. As in flower design, cluster types together to make a display with a central theme or colour scheme.

Fruit boxes and trays from the market can be lined with leaves to make inexpensive containers. A harvest basket lined with a checked table napkin brings a picnic flavour to the table.

A Celebration Tray brightens up the long hours of a convalescent who is temporarily immobile but not restricted to a special diet. This summery tray of champagne and seafood is guaranteed to tempt a jaded appetite and

bring back memories of better times.

The delicate spray of sugar-frosted red currants adds a frivolous note to the glass, but a more personal touch might be a single flower.

Serving food on leaves has a long tradition and a tiny

portion of mussels treated in this way is just the sort of encouragement to put patients back on their feet. Nasturtium flowers add a colourful touch and are also edible.

Taking plain ingredients and presenting them imaginatively is a challenge; well-tried family recipes can be given a lift when garnished with flowers.

Vegetables and Desserts

VEGETABLES AS A CENTERPIECE can form a dramatic, yet low-key, table decoration. Aim for contrasting shapes and textures, matching the scale of the components and harmonizing the colours. Keep the proportions under control and relate the design to the colour and feeling of the food and occasion. If in expansive mood, seek inspiration from oriental temple decorations in which fruit, vegetables and flowers are piled high to form tall obelisks or pyramids of festive colour.

Lush asparagus tied with purple ribbon forms the center of this display. It rises from a bed of artichokes and endive salad, all of the colours subtly toning. Linen table napkins have been starched and folded into water-lily points, their crisp shapes contrasting with the curly leaves of endive.

When using vegetables for table decoration, ensure that they are thoroughly washed and dried; "groom" them by removing any soiled or torn leaves and, after preparation, keep them in a cool place until required.

Grouping material of widely differing shapes can create a new "species" of flower. For example, tuck a few summer flowers in and around cabbage leaves in a basket or wedge bundles of wild grass, held with a rubber band, into a bowl of fruit or vegetables, letting them sway in graceful curves with every passing breeze. A collection of green or yellow gourds on a wooden platter can be enhanced with single flower heads scattered throughout or simply a single bloom acting as a focal point—a design technique to help the arrangement from looking too busy.

THE DESSERT STAGE of a meal is an ideal opportunity to show off your decorative skills. Your choice of china, lighting, flowers and the dessert itself can all interact to make a splendid show. Flickering candlelight here sparkles from the gold rim of the lower serving plate; fresh flowers are tucked into the fruit and the crowning glory is the dessert itself—an appetizing fruit *feuilleté* with feathered *crème Anglaise*.

Whether the dessert is presented as individual servings or as a single centerpiece, it is one of the most decorative parts of the meal. Using plates with painted flower and fruit designs adds another dimension to floral decoration. Dessert trolleys in restaurants often display imaginative pastries and cheeses. Old-fashioned cookbooks, such as Mrs. Beeton's, indulge in the art of pastry decoration, edible lattice and flowers, and spun-sugar confections. This approach may be a little Victorian for modern taste, but it is a starting point to inspire your own dishes.

Fanciful arrangements of fruit, pastries and tartlets can be made for the side table. Imagine a basic pattern such as a fanshape, lattice or diagonal bands, a checkerboard, maze or circular pattern; then build the individual delicacies into the chosen shape, linking colour and form. The overall effect can be dramatically increased by the scale, reflected in a lacquer or silver tray. But a large oval serving platter, a flat round basket tray or a tiered china cake stand can all be used in the same way, with an occasional flower tucked into the design.

Salad Days

EDIBLE PETALS AND LEAVES in a glass lotus bowl add a new dimension to salad luncheons. A few bowls of salad foliage, of different colours and textures, give an appetizing choice at party time. Red cabbage, Chinese leaves and dark red nasturtium flowers make a dramatic salad. Or use yellow and orange nasturtium petals with clusters of fresh green lettuce. All sorts of colour schemes can be made—yellow and green peppers with tomatoes and basil, purple pansies in a green salad with celery, or marigold petals and purple sage leaves. Common herbs, such as mint, parsley and thyme, spice up a salad and lemon slices add freshness to the dish.

AN EXOTIC CULINARY "FLOWER" can be created with a clutch of quail's eggs, nestled on lettuce leaves arranged like curly petals atop a bed of bright green sea oxeye. A magpie touch is added to this nest arrangement by the insertion of a summer daisy.

Nests can be made from all kinds of leaves, daisy flower heads or wafer cookies. The culinary "flower" can then be arranged directly on the nest or rising out of it on a pedestal platter.

There are several cookbooks available that specialize in garden salads and decorative food presentation. They may encourage you to start exploring new ideas, new ingredients and new flavours.

Since ingredients may not be available all year round, you will have to be creative in thinking of fresh colourful dishes—all green fruits, for example, or a salad in various shades of red, including red-veined cheeses, grated beets, radishes and red beans.

61

Living Rooms

Extending flower arranging beyond its usual decorative role is a creative challenge and will add a new dimension to your home. By making the flowers interact with their surroundings, you enhance the design of your living space.

Flowers can be used in a variety of ways. They can be used as a screen, subtly dividing a room. With colour in mind, you can link the flowers with textured upholstery, tapestry or a picture on the wall and translate the three-dimensional arrangement into a reinterpretation of the artistic theme, using the colours of the plant material as an artist would use those on his palette. Value flowers that are in season, letting them fall in soft cascades with natural grace.

In a romantic vein, flowers can be used as souvenirs of happy times, a garden stroll or a weekend picnic. The scent of a single rose is as evocative of summer as a whole bouquet. Arrangements also work well in tiny vases, placed here and there around the room.

Reflected images in mirror glass or other shiny surfaces, whether in sharp or soft focus, double the scale of a design. You can create a "free" arrangement this way or experiment with repeating patterns of flower units, making an unusual total effect.

By choosing a container that suggests a certain style, by interpreting a special occasion in flowers or by expanding on a theme, "doing the flowers" becomes something much more than simply home decorating.

AN ELEGANT LIVING ROOM is glimpsed through a delicate screen of anthuriums. The graceful line of each is clearly apparent, rising as if from nothing above a glass-topped table. The vase reveals the pattern of crossing stems from which the flowers fountain upwards.

Placed in the center of the room, the flowers draw a rosy veil between the ends without creating the slightest sense of division. The flaglike anthuriums flutter against the landscape in the picture beyond, and create a feeling of spaciousness.

The Floral Screen

FLOWERS USED AS A SCREEN create a visual partition. Three flutes of an epergne launch a firework of flowers and stems, with the carnations exploding in a shower against the light. Shiny dark green ivy leaves encircle the rim of each flute like a pointed collar.

The vase-life of the flowers can be extended by removing dead blooms and cutting the stems short as the new buds open. Arranged in the same container, these create tight rosettes of colour.

AN ABSTRACT SCREENLIKE QUALITY is created with stems. The Rouault portrait behind seems to be imprisoned by the swelling stems, the pompon flower heads culminating at the man's eye level.

Minimal plant material, imaginatively handled, brings a surreal humour to the arrangement, suggesting that the allium stems rise like elongated stoppers topped by their own globes. Stems are placed in heavy glass decanters and bottles filled with water at different levels.

GLITTERING GLASS as a setting is reminiscent of a Fabergé jewel, the gypsophila forming a galaxy behind the full moon of a single rose. The sharp outline of the leaves adds a shadowy dimension, important in an all-white arrangement.

In Japanese floral art, the essence of a landscape may be depicted by a single branch of blossom in a bowl of water. Once the imagination is set free, the pleasure of making a simple arrangement is doubled. Here a few flowers, some water and clarity of glass are touched with light, creating a scene like a flurry of snow-flakes on a windowpane.

The sparkling beauty of glass and water is revealed by light. A modern glass vase is filled with water in which chunks of crystal are submerged. These rough pieces of glass support the flower stems while accentuating the play of light through the transparency of the container and emphasizing the purity of white flowers.

Creating Visual Links

THE FUN OF LINKING FLOWERS to other decorative features is stimulating; colour, texture, shape and pattern can be your inspiration. In an interview in 1954, Matisse summed up this idea: "A painting on a wall should be like a bouquet of flowers in an interior."

Works of art are used here on equal terms with a minimalist floral line-up—flowers of related colours live well with artworks. A plaster sculpture of a vase of flowers links with the real flowers beneath it: Gerbera heads individually arranged. These are set against a backdrop of an oil crayon design in colourful arcs and angular strokes, while the Clarice Cliff plates introduce an additional bold pattern.

THE RICH MOSAIC of stitches in the tapestry chair seat have inspired the colour and texture of this floral basket arrangement. Heathers form a rounded bunch, set in a bowl inside the basket. Bicolour parrot tulips with frilled petals are placed within the bouquet. One or two stems deliberately left longer throw the spherical shape a little off balance. The result is a graceful variation of outline with an element of surprise.

The soft pastel colouring accords well with the pale fruitwood furniture. The natural arrangement retains the delicacy of flowers fresh from the garden.

EMBROIDERY from an antique Chinese robe has been framed for a modern interior. The anemones, flowing with the sinuous lines of an Alvar Åalto glass vase, are faintly reflected in the shiny green plastic of the table. The wavy lines of intense flower colour are seemingly framed in the rectangle of the fireplace and its reflection—a three-dimensional version of the picture on the wall.

Undulating bands of embroidery are the inspiration for "painting with flowers." The gaily coloured petals and black stamens of the anemones duplicate the strong colours of the oriental silks.

The anemones are first loosely gathered in colour bunches, from white and pink through red to purple, and placed in the container. Then the flowers are gently shuffled so that they glide in a continuous river of colour.

Decorative Harmony

INTIMATE MINI ARRANGEMENTS— mementos of a walk in the garden, the last flower from a bouquet, the first violets— placed on a bureau or dressing table give private moments of pleasure. Vita Sackville-West always had on her writing desk at Sissinghurst the first flowers as they bloomed, separately arranged as single heads or tiny bunches. This idea can easily be extended to the kitchen, dining room and bathroom.

A single daffodil rests in an old glass inkwell, a cluster of snowdrops at shelf-level and a favourite Galle vase holds a single branch of pussy willow, under the watchful eye of a distant relative.

The swirling organic pattern of leaves and honeysuckle in the William Morris wallpaper invites the use of flowers with similar panache. Once you are receptive to the decorative features all around, choosing and arranging flowers to interpret an idea can be linked with textiles and colours, and to your favourite things.

PAIRS OF VASES, besides being treated in the same way at either end of a mantelpiece, can stand side by side, each repeating the architectural quality of the other.

These distinctly coloured glass vases are used very differently. The tulip buds are bunched and their stems cut to form a sculptural element growing out of the rich dark tones of the glass. They are strongly illuminated from above as if the tabletop were a stage. The light accentuates their roundness and makes them glow. The partner vase stands tall with a single slender long-stemmed iris and the shield of a tulip leaf. Both arrangements are distinct against the black lacquer cabinet in the background.

A PAIRED INFORMALITY is created with vases of different size and shape. The foreground is dominated by two containers, related neither in size nor in form. The larger vase features alstroemeria in a natural arrangement which balances visually with the tulip buds beyond. Lily-of-the-valley contributes the extra element of perfume to the arrangement.

Lighting plays a vital role in the interrelationship of these four vases. The largest has a loose style, the flowers strongly lit from one side, light and shade creating a decorative silhouette against the wall. The lily-of-the-valley is a highlight in this chiaroscuro. The four individual designs, all very different in character, work together in decorative harmony with their surroundings.

69

Unabashed Graphics

A HALF-MOON drop shelf opens to facilitate the making of cocktails in this '30s cocktail cabinet. A pair of crescent-shaped vases is placed one slightly behind the other to create a recurring semicircular theme linking cabinet, vases and the Sonia Delaunay painting on the wall.

The vase in front is an off-balance arrangement of laurel leaves and anemones; the second vase contains a stand of yellow irises in bud, all cut to the same length. These have great textural quality and the stems add a strong upright pattern.

Vases in pairs can be used effectively side by side or staggered one behind the other in a recurring theme. The more decorative and unusual the vases' shape, the more graphically exciting the arrangement. The vases themselves are as much part of the design as the flowers.

Charity stores and rummage sales sometimes offer such vases, considered by many people as being impossible for flower display. But used confidently, in a graphic way, such vases look special and create a strong personal note.

THE COCKTAIL CABINET is a busy spot in any living room with hardly any space for flowers. A simple arrangement is a tall glass vase holding two anthurium flowers and a leaf high above the level of bottles and decanters. The effect is clean, simple and uncluttered, and the plants seem to float above the tabletop in airy detachment.

Although the flowers in this design do not weigh much, it is always advisable to place such a tall arrangement in a vase with a heavy base so that it will not topple over. Alternatively, pebbles or fine sand can be used to weight the container and, incidentally, provide an additional feature of the design, seen in magnified form through the transparent glass.

Looking-Glass Themes

MIRROR, GLASS, PLASTIC, METAL OR LACQUER—all reflect flowers in a surface beyond the arrangement and serve to extend the impact of the design.

In Japanese garden design, water reflections play a vital role in creating mood and mystery. Look for this same quality in the reflective surfaces of a modern living room. Reflections bring the room to life. A passing cloud beyond a nearby window, a person moving across a room, changing light patterns—all bring movement. Using

flowers to "echo" such movements, however softly, in a reflective or highly polished surface, gives life to the whole arrangement.

Mirrors double the size, making big arrangements even bigger in scale and thus more impressive. Mirror glass is the clearest and most effective reflective surface used in the decoration of walls and, with discretion, it can create an illusion of space. Mirrors are not commonly used on table tops today, but the fashionable appeal of Art Deco, in which mirrored surfaces work with enormous success, may influence designs of the future.

Plastic, glass and lacquers reflect in a softer, more shadowy way, showing less

distinct form and colour.

The translucent reflections in a modern glass-topped table (*above*) create a mood of cool elegance. The glass pedestal vase is placed to appear as if at the feet of the young man in the painting on the wall. The flowers are arranged in a

romantic free form: White camellias are added as small accents to a bouquet picked from the garden, glimpsed beyond the window. The height of the vase allows the gypsophila to hang in a cloud below the sunny flowers. Garden blooms falling in graceful curves about a classical container can be studied in the masterly flower paintings of Fantin-Latour.

A PROFUSION of brightly coloured croton leaves makes up this exotic foliage arrangement. Its placement in front of a large mirror doubles the impact of the huge bunch to give the impression of a golden bush of shiny leaves.

The equally exotic enameled container is decorated with oriental birds and blossom painted on a chrome-yellow background. By placing a special container against a mirror, you can see the whole design and can appreciate the "phantom vase of flowers" with equal pleasure.

Accessories flanking the vase have been carefully chosen to link in colour and veracity with the oriental feeling transposed to a western environment. Potted plants fill the empty fireplace with colour and a tall ceramic vase on the side table beyond balances out the room.

BASKETS OF FLOWERS appear to float like paper boats when seen in the abstract patterns of shadows created by the play of window light on a shiny plastic table.

The flowers are selected to contrast or harmonize in hue with their containers. To enjoy the development of the design over several days, the flowers are arranged initially at the bud stage, the colours expanding to fill each dish as they mature. Iris buds placed in one basket burst open to spangle the Victorian glass container with gold spikes. Similarly, the purple anemones become more densely packed as the petals open, the flowers in their final glory a celebration of pure colour.

Curls, Swirls and Twists

THE SWIRLS of the wall painting are repeated in the glass curls incorporated into the design of a translucent Lalique vase. The thrust of a giant bud of a *Monstera deliciosa* playfully indicates the painted curls as if to continue the scribble design. The arrangement is completed by a spray of finely cut croton foliage, dark and twisted.

A GAME OF CONTRAST is played by placing a small bowl arrangement from a nearby coffee table alongside the normally solo performance of the major design behind. Secondary placements moved about the room, to make space for a tray for example, can introduce an interplay of entirely different arrangements, setting them off against each other and drawing attention to their individuality, which is in no way diminished by contrast. Differing styles put together by chance take on a surprising affinity and open up fresh design possibilities.

THE CORRUGATED TEXTURE of the wall covering forms a backdrop to the dramatic swirling design of the painting. Its white space is brightly lit, bringing the arching patterns into strong focus to balance the latticed radiator cover on which the arrangement stands—a truly 1980s interior.

Huge variegated leaves of New Zealand flax make strong brushlike strokes across canvas and continue the graphic lines of the design. The flax is supported by sprays of scarlet helicona, the crisscrossed pattern of its sturdy stems magnified through the column of clear glass. Marble obelisks stand like exclamation marks as if to emphasize the drama of the plant material.

This arrangement was made in summer, but remember most flowers will wilt quickly if placed above heated radiator panels. Exotic foliage such as this is resilient to central heating and lasts for long periods in clean water. But, as a general guide, fresh flowers are best kept away from hot air currents.

A REPEATING PATTERN of single stems, all arching and pointing in the same direction, makes an effective modern display. You can even draw attention to the end of the line where some special object could be placed.

Specimen vases, each containing a single flowering stem or leaf, have their own graphic quality. The natural rhythm of the stems, the silhouette of the flower heads, the movement of the line—all create an impression of silent music, a marching arabesque of shapes and spaces.

By changing the distance between vases or their relative position and angle, a whole new "score" can be created. All types of flowers and leaves can be arranged in this way to give a special effect. The plant material takes on a completely new look when isolated thus; all manner of patterns and textures become apparent which are not usually seen when the material is set in a more formal traditional style.

The firm strokes of the freesias here play a rhythmic theme in tune with the swirling patterns of the painting behind. The water level in each vase varies and the strong arch of the stems is augmented by repetition.

Flowers of the same colour can be used, or different colours in each container to make a toning scheme. Shorter stems emphasize the flower heads while long stems create more movement. The proportions of the design depend on the position and the effect you wish to create. But remember, the longer the stems, the more important it is to check the weighting of the vase to ensure it will not topple over.

Repeating Movements

STRONG GRAPHIC STATEMENTS are made by displaying single dramatic leaves each in their own container. These brightly coloured, veined croton leaves make a bold arrangement, leaping along like a school of humpback whales. Your attention is held by their glossy texture and streamlined shape. The effect would be dissipated if the leaves were obscured in a more random arrangement.

Nature provides many wonderful shapes, textures and colours, so use them to make uninhibited and inventive statements.

Exotic Collections

EXUBERANT FLOWERS and container are linked by colour with their surroundings. The lively pink and yellow colour scheme of this city apartment is matched by the designer vase and its casual bouquet. The flowers were loosely bunched in the hand, then placed in the vase. By gently lifting them and allowing them to fall in a natural way, a relaxed effect is created. This complements the seeming spontaneity of the hand-crafted container.

AN AIRY COLLECTION of greenery brings the outdoors inside. Grasses and leaves blend in an uninhibited "disarranged arrangement," which "borrows" foliage from the garden beyond and brings it into close focus. The lightness and simplicity of this arrangement, made in a large jug, is inspired by the way in which plants grow and interweave in their natural environment.

A HALL TABLE takes on a
Mexican desert theme,
inspired by the paintings of
Georgia O'Keeffe and her
home in New Mexico. The
muted colours and brittle
character of this design are
intended to bring to mind the
bleached aridity of a Mexican
landscape.

A deer skull, decorated with
floral "eyes," overlooks a
crowded tablescape of smooth
pebbles, rough pottery and
prickly cacti. There is great

contrast in the shapes, colours
and textures of this
arrangement. The rounded
shapes of the pebbles, piled
one on top of the other, and of
the cacti are repeated in the
pumpkin, which is balanced
on a tile. Dried veronica,
loosely bunched in a clay jar,
and montbretia, with spiky
leaves, echo the shape of the
antlers on the wall. A rusty fish
kettle provides a container for
a collection of smaller cacti.

Interpreting a Theme

THE PICASSO VASE is the inspiration for this arrangement. The vase itself can be interpreted in two ways, either as a fawn with horns or as an owl with staring eyes and wings. The vase's handles can suggest either the horns or the wings. Picasso's work is given a third meaning by the addition of a headdress of flowers. Topped with antennae of alliums and a circlet of lilies and arums, the vase takes on the figure of a mythological god. Picasso would be amused.

IN WRY CONTRAST to the sculpture by Picasso, a primitive pottery self-portrait container crafted by a schoolboy is decorated with plant material to imitate a punk hairdo; green leaves form a bizarre "Mohican" style, dressed with a single daffodil. Placed on the child's desk, it conveys a message—"have a nice day" or "have I surprised you?"

The Picasso vase is fitted with its own metal cone which rests inside the neck of the vase and protects it when using florist's foam. But you do not necessarily need a priceless container to enjoy making an amusing commentary on flower art.

TOURIST CARVINGS can often lose their glamour when taken from their native surroundings and placed in the more mundane atmosphere of the home. But these African figures, like Giacometti sculptures, can be made to tell a story with a little creative flower work.

Group the figures in a line, dance them in a circle or stand them back to back. An assortment of leaves and grasses is appropriate for foliage has always been adopted for camouflage or for tribal ceremonial. Here the leaves represent banners, shields, spears and trophies. The figures stand bow-legged on a tray of woven grass.

The stems are kept fresh in water-filled glass tubes, sealed with rubber stoppers. Each figure is decorated with a crossbelt of raffia into which are tucked the leaves.

Baroque Elegance

A SET OF FOUR CRAFT VASES of classical form are decorated with unusual repeating motifs. Linked together as a group along two adjoining console tables, they share a baroque theme of three-dimensional cherubs on trumpet-shaped containers.

In the first arrangement, parrot tulips are bunched in the hand and then placed in the vase to fall into a relaxed position, producing a "non-arranged" casual look.

The red and green architectural theme is the inspiration for choosing these flowers to form a curly ionic "capital" to complement the Greek motif of the vase.

CHERUBS PLAY under a sweep of soft roses mixed with bicolour tulips in a bold cascade of colour. One tulip springs out of the design in a graceful arc and a single leaf has floated down to rest on a cherub's back.

Such a vase seems almost to dictate the way in which flowers look best and gives enormous pleasure to the arranger.

LILIES ARE ARRANGED in a manner reminiscent of Renaissance altar paintings, the flowers set full-face and in profile to display all aspects of their form. The twisting movement of the lilies arises directly from the spiral pattern on the vase. The black and white motif is gently recreated in the silhouette of the leaves. Flowers and foliage are deliberately blended in a mass of texture out of which individual blooms spring into focus.

A single orange streak of colour provides a strong visual link between all four designs.

BAROQUE ANGELS in a swirl of ceramic drapery float past a *faux* marble column. This vase inspired an asymmetrical design, its moody earth colours prompting the choice of heathers and a cloud of olive-green foliage. Greenish-yellow buds of daffodils shine like jewels against the textured background of fine leaves and starry gypsophila.

It is fun to create a rhythm of movement between the arrangements. A strong individual character has been imparted to each of these four vases.

Shelving

Mantelpieces, bookcases, windowsills, tops of cabinets, steps, ledges — flat surfaces of varying widths and heights abound in every home and give shelf-room for displays of flowers alongside your favourite possessions. Treat a shelf as a miniature stage, an ideal exhibition area, but exercise a little discipline to avoid clutter. You don't need to put all your favourite things on one shelf at the same time; bring out a few and experiment with matching or toning schemes, then make your flower designs interact with the overall scheme you choose.

An arrangement on a shelf is seen in close association with the objects immediately surrounding it, whether these are books, a mirror or painting on the wall behind, or a backdrop of patterned wallpaper. The width of the shelf, its height, position and surroundings must therefore be taken into account when planning your floral scheme. "Shelf-traffic" must also be considered; an elaborate display on a much-used bookshelf, for example, will become a nuisance. Narrow shelves call for "thin" arrangements, while broad shelves can carry displays, even extravaganzas.

Lighting can be orchestrated to achieve different effects with shelf displays. The whole concept of a design can be changed by the type of lighting used and by the angle from which the light comes — above, below or from the side. Arrangements on glass shelves are particularly effective when lit well.

The fireplace is often the focal point in a room and flowers set on the mantelpiece are perfectly positioned for attention. It is not necessary to have an arrangement in the center; asymmetrical placements, unusual containers and ornaments that are conversation pieces make arrangements on shelves much more interesting.

AN OIL PAINTING above a marble mantelpiece, which is set with art objects, has a formality that can lead to a static, even unimaginative, scene. But by making the painting, ornaments and flowers interact to tell a story, you can create a real point of interest in the room.

The first lilies of the season move here in rhythm with the Frank Auerbach painting behind, while the wings of stylized doves add to this powerful white-on-white design. By placing the flowers in simple everyday containers, the informality of the design comes across. The central flower is cut to a length that makes it appear to spring out of the painting. The posy adds a final whimsical touch.

Two by Two

A PAIR OF VASES, overflowing with a mass of fluttering sweet peas, decorates the narrow shelf above the fireplace. An amusing illusion is created by placing postcard reproductions of museum pieces in front of the real containers, to give the impression of priceless vases on your mantelpiece. The fact that the "vases" and their flowers are wildly out of proportion to each other does not matter — it is an entertaining visual game.

INTEGRATED DESIGN makes a powerful composition. This symmetrical arrangement of curving cornucopias in pairs, set against the sinewy lines of the Empire snake mirror, draws your attention to the central area, where an African ceremonial mask is placed. Such a combination of matching containers, art objects and flowers makes for a unified design theme. This theme can be used effectively in the hallway or on a side table in the living or dining room. The floral theme in the three pairs of vases here consists of loosely bunched posies of freesias and snowdrops.

IDENTICAL GLASS CUBES hold bunches of carnations, set at an angle which seems to defy gravity. Like two exotic birds, one tipped with purple, the flowers rise out of crystal-clear water. White pebbles decorate the inside of the vases and are brilliantly reflected in the smoky glass tabletop.

The flowers were bunched in the hand and their stems then wedged between the pebbles for support. By using identical containers, there is no distraction from the main floral theme, the variation here comes from the flowers themselves.

Shelves Galore

BLENDING THE NEUTRAL COLOURS in the Patrick Procktor painting with the hessian-covered walls brings a restful air to the fireplace, the focal point of the room. But add a dash of surprise with a mass of bright flowers, combining the colours of the rainbow, in a shimmering informal design. Balance is achieved by placing the vase off-center, visually opposite the white forms in the picture. The eucalyptus leaves act as a colour link between the greys of the painting and the veins in the marble of the mantelpiece.

INDIVIDUAL FLOWER HEADS make a simple display on two shelves; set singly like this, the precise sculpture of each bloom is more easily appreciated. Each flower is valued as a single unit and also as part of the total design. There is a naïve, almost childlike quality in such an arrangement.

Assorted coffee cups and liqueur glasses are perfect containers for individual flowers. The oval plate forms a visual bond between the three cups on the upper shelf. A carnation overflows from one cup, the petals of a lily lick the rim of another, and the third cup complements the splash of yellow in the iris petals.

On the shelf below, the glasses are seen both as a quartet and as a double pair of red and yellow arrangements. One pair is raised on a box to link it visually with the shelf above. The glass becomes almost invisible and the flowers seem to float against the white wall.

FOCUS ATTENTION on favourite objects, such as books and ornaments, by using them as part of a floral design. The black crystal specimen vases here are camouflaged against the rich leather bindings of the books and they complement the Herculean bookends. The freesias appear as brush-drawn dabs of colour above a fine mist of stippled gypsophila. Such an arrangement can be made from individual stems saved from a bunch of flowers past its prime.

Dried flowers can be displayed on the uppermost shelves of a bookcase. They need little care and will be out of the way, yet they form most effective displays, their rich earthy colours blending with the bindings. Fresh hydrangeas are good value because they can be dried *in situ* and, as the weeks go by, their colours change from pastel blues and pinks to dusky purples and soft beiges.

Flowers at the Window

A COPPER PITCHER holds a bouquet of tulips, bathed in spring sunlight on a country cottage windowsill. Splashes of red and yellow are reflected in the polished metal and enhance its mellow tones. Autumnal shades also look well in copper and brass containers.

Two china dishes filled with dried artichokes provide a textural contrast to the smoothness of the tulip heads and pitcher. A giant pine cone echoes the shape of the artichokes. As the light changes during the day, so do the patterns created by the flowers and their complementary ornaments.

When night comes and the curtains are closed, the stage is set for the table below the window, which has remained in shadow for much of the day. Now a still life of dried helichrysum in a polished tankard with a basket of fruit alongside become apparent. The whole scene is lit with warm artificial light.

A WINDOW IS FRAMED with an arrangement of white china, vases and gelatin molds chosen for their drapelike forms, which give a curtained effect to the window. Delicate tulips flow from the ceramic gelatin mold, with the upright stems of daffodils visually linking the pine trees in the garden beyond. Natural light bathes the windowsill display in a soft haze. The outline of the white petals melts into the sky.

The arrangement is threaded through a base of pine branches and larch, which acts as a framework to support the flowers.

THE OLD-WORLD CHARM of leaded glass, whitewashed walls and a deep windowsill create a country feel and link the outdoors and indoors.

Colours can be varied according to the season, changing from spring bulbs to summer roses through to autumn leaves and berries. But the all-white arrangement is always effective and very much part of a contemporary "white loves white" style of decoration.

Above Eye-level

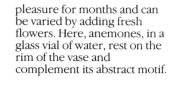

THE INLAID PANELS of Chinese calligraphy inspired this arrangement of four unmatched containers of green glass. The flowers were chosen to echo the ancient script and they form a further series of graphic characters.

A MORE CONTRIVED INTERPRETATION shows another way in which flowers can be used to express an idea. A golden "rod of lightning," consisting of yellow blossom braided with raffia in a zig-zag pattern, is angled into the vase so as to strike its red target. The design mimics the high-kicking figure on the piano.

THE STRONG ARCHITECTURAL lines of a Biedermeier chest contrast with the rounded shape of the handcrafted container. Dried flowers, placed above eye-level, give pleasure for months and can be varied by adding fresh flowers. Here, anemones, in a glass vial of water, rest on the rim of the vase and complement its abstract motif.

CONTINUING THE CHINESE THEME, the flowing lines of broom and heather (*right*) echo the delicate picture on the inlaid black lacquer cabinet. The shape of the iris mirrors that of the bird below and the white rose seems to be part of the painting behind. The flowers are contained within the gilt frame of the painting, while the eye links the various levels of display in a three-dimensional scheme.

Placing flowers in front of a painting does hide it from view, but only temporarily; when the arrangement is removed, the painting can be seen again and perhaps appreciated in a fresh light.

Bedrooms

Small and intimate arrangements are appropriate for a bedroom, which is usually a private place. Sweet peas, spring flowers, single bud arrangements or small clusters of wild grasses are good bedroom flowers. Delicate, relaxed, easy-on-the-eye—these are the kinds of display you want to wake up to on your bedside table.

The guest bedroom may require something more stirring; match the flowers to the person and the mood of the occasion. Interesting objects on the bedside table also add a thoughtful touch. A wall vase in a dressing room is ideal for a buttonhole, a tiny nosegay or a sachet of potpourri. But most of all, your flowers should be a personal message of welcome to your guest, chosen and arranged with care. Similarly for someone who is sick or convalescing, a small arrangement is a reminder of the garden outside, an incentive to recovery.

There are many accessories in a bedroom to which the flowers can be linked in form and colour—the bedspread, sheets, table lamp, wallpaper, paintings, dresser. Matching patterns and flowers, or contrasting them for effect, can give much pleasure and will be evident in the thoughtful result.

A bathroom *en suite* can also be linked to the bedroom through the flowers, although the textural surfaces and atmosphere of the rooms are different. A bathroom mirror, reflecting back into the bedroom, is an effective way of relating flower themes and colours in the two rooms.

A DRESSING TABLE can be intimate, practical and decorative all at the same time. Flowers add to those private moments spent in front of the looking glass.

Elegance is the message of a tall glass vase in which a large heart-shaped hosta leaf anchors an arch of lily leaves, curving above a flutter of orchids in a silver and crystal pot. Balancing the white and green theme is a minimalist test tube with a few grasses and a single spray of nicotiana, whose stems complete the design.

Bedside Surprises

AN OPTICAL ILLUSION is created by propping a postcard of a Chinese vase in front of the actual container, a plain glass jar. A surreal quality is lent to the tabletop with its assortment of items in different colours, patterns and textures. Sweet peas flutter like butterflies above the "museum piece" vase and complement its flowery pattern. The whole illusion is fun; any picture can be used, maybe a London Beefeater to remind you of a visit to the Tower, or the Statue of Liberty.

TO WELCOME A GUEST, place flowers by the bedside. The scale of the arrangement is not important—a single stem is as effective as a whole bouquet. But to add a personal touch, a thoughtful scheme might combine a cluster of golden pears and a small display of different flowers grouped to create a sculptural design. Your guest is greeted with a pleasing composition, a light perfume and the fruits of summer.

The tulip is cut short and maximum attention given to its shield-shaped leaf. The perfumed rose rests on the rim of a handmade vase, almost oriental in feeling. And the eucalyptus silhouette makes a delicate contrast to the rounded shapes of the flowers.

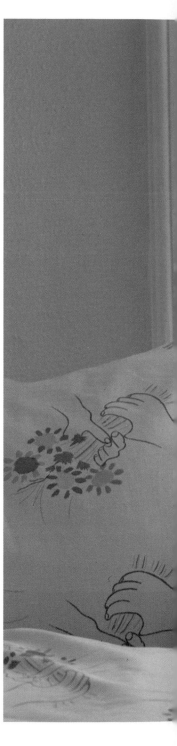

MORNING LIGHT filters through this fresh arrangement placed on a pine chest of drawers by the bed. The floral theme is continued on the sheets, decorated with a Picasso print of a hand holding a bunch of flowers. A few pieces of a Clarice Cliff morning set complete the picture of country living.

The flowers, selected for their unusual relationship to each other, are placed in a glass wine carafe, which is given a special touch by an organza handkerchief trimming. Gathering the material into a small knot at the center with a rubber band, slip the band over the neck of the vase and gently tease the material into four points to hang like transparent petals. The arrangement was made in the hand, the stems then cut to length and placed in the carafe. An airy effect, like a halo, surrounds the display.

Get Well Soon

BLENDING ART AND REALITY, full-blown roses interact with an embroidered shawl hung on the bedroom wall. The coloured marbles filling the glass vases enhance the effect against the exotic backdrop of birds and flowers.

The roses have changed during their vase-life from buds to full blooms, adding a dimension of continuing interest, ideal beside a patient's bed where long hours may be spent in solitude.

To support a single stem in this way, half-fill the vase with marbles or pebbles, then position the rose and gently continue filling the vase. Finally, top up with water, ensuring that the level is maintained over the next few days.

"THE BELOVED," a painting by the Pre-Raphaelite Dante Gabriel Rossetti, inspired this cylindrical basket of flowers.

Roses and cornflowers make up a seasonal bouquet in which the stems are cut to a length slightly longer than the height of the basket, then arranged in the hand to form a close mound of perfumed blooms. Grasses fill the spaces between, bringing a touch of whimsy to the sturdiness of the arrangement.

The light scent of garden flowers is always welcome in the bedroom, but especially at the bedside of someone who is ill. Heavily perfumed flowers can give a heady, cloying atmosphere. Some other suggestions for hospital flowers are given on p. 133.

A MISCELLANEOUS COLLECTION of small treasures presented to a convalescing patient gives hours of lasting pleasure when visitors are gone. Smooth pebbles and shells of varied hues give visual and tactile pleasure, and can also bring back pleasant memories of seaside vacations.

The flowers are gathered with the same care, a pretty reminder of the garden outside. The arrangement is presented on a tray with the addition of succulent green and black grapes.

A point of interest is added by a spray of *Dicentra spectabilis* whose flowers hang like tiny lockets on a chain, ready to disclose "the lady in the bath" should the patient feel curious enough to tease the petals gently aside.

Bathrooms

The bathroom is often the most neglected room in the house for flower displays. And yet the setting is ideal; flowers flourish in its steamy atmosphere and reflections in tiled and mirrored surfaces multiply images and form a perfect backdrop. Time spent in the bathroom is supposed to be relaxing, time off to lounge in a warm soapy tub, wash your hair, do your make-up, have a leisurely shave. The presence of flowers invites you to relax.

There are many levels in a bathroom where flowers can be placed to advantage—shelves, sink and bath surrounds. In any position, you can enjoy close-up or eye-level contact with fresh arrangements, or even admire them standing free in a corner of the room.

It is fun to experiment with bathroom containers for flowers—soap holders, shaving mugs, old make-up pots can be used to great effect. The whole colour scheme of the room can be enlivened with brightly coloured flowers, making the bathroom a place in which you will enjoy spending time.

GOOD MORNING, SUNSHINE! Daffodils are cut to stand with their heads just emerging over the rim of a 1930s Art Deco vase to make a dome of pure gold. The texture of the curly petals contrasts with the geometric patterns of the ceramic container and the checkerboard tiles. The shiny surfaces of the tiles and the vase, with the light striking it at an angle, together with the mirrored image of the flowers, all combine to make this a bold graphic arrangement, featuring different colours, shapes and textures.

Mirror Images

A NOTE OF FANTASY is lent to this ceramic swan with an arrangement of lilac, laurel leaves, water grasses and a single tulip nestled on its back.

The swan seems to glide over the surface, with tail feathers of grasses and wings of laurel spread. Using the imagination to interpret such a design gives a fun dimension to flower arranging.

NARROW SHELVES and shatter-proof plastic containers go together, especially above a sink or bath where breakages might cause injury.

Amaryllis flowers make a good show, but their heavy heads and sturdy stem need

firm support. The transparent container has been filled with attractive shells and sand, which add weight to the container and also serve to wedge the stem firmly in place. The frill of mussel shells adds an amusing touch.

A LOW-LEVEL POSITION for these small irises allows you to admire them from above or at close quarters when in the bath. The flowers are held loosely in place by small stones and are reflected in the water of the plastic container, like a miniature lake scene.

These small irises have an exquisite scent, which will waft throughout the bathroom. Orris root is extracted from irises and is used in powdered form to perfume potpourri. The ancient Greeks used it to perfume their bed linen. Irises also have the advantage of coming in many colour varieties and this allows you to match the flowers to the colour scheme of your bathroom.

A WALL MIRROR doubles the image of an arrangement set on a shelf above the sink. The unusual vase, crafted as a blackamoor's head, is adorned with a ceremonial headdress of gypsophila, tulips, alstroemeria and irises.

Vase and flowers combine in a whimsical design, which can be appreciated from above and in close-up, as well as in its reflection beyond.

Reflective Themes

A JUNGLE EFFECT can be created in a small area by grouping bowls of contrasting foliage, ferns and water grasses together, with cut flowers added as a highlight. Personal items scattered around give a welcoming air sometimes lacking in modern bathrooms where streamlined design features may not encourage you to linger.

ROSES make good company anywhere, but their perfume is a particular delight when you are relaxing in the bath. Picked from the garden when the buds are half open, they will soon blossom in the warm atmosphere of the bathroom. This bunch is clustered in a goldfish bowl whose shape complements their full heads.

A CERAMIC toothbrush holder is a simple container for a simple arrangement of four flowers fresh from the garden. Busy people seldom have time to examine individual flowers, but placed on the side of the bath, they can be regarded at leisure.

LEFTOVERS from other arrangements about the house are perfect for the bathroom. Flower heads inadvertently broken are saved for a small glass vase, which is placed on a scalloped soapdish to provide a delicate touch.

A PAIR of pottery craft jugs with a metallic glaze link marble, chrome and white ceramic surfaces in a scheme of bathroom neutrals.

An array of lilies, irises and tulips makes an airy design with its own pattern of spaces silhouetted against the wall. By spacing the flowers in the vases, each petal and stem becomes apparent, matching the simple elegance of the studio pottery.

Kitchens

Flowers in the kitchen cheer up a working area which is generally planned on strictly utilitarian lines. But the kitchen should also be a welcoming room, where family and friends come together to eat and talk and while away the hours in warmth and comfort. Flowers, brightly coloured and simply arranged, create an atmosphere of welcome, bringing the garden into the home.

There are all sorts of unusual containers you can make use of in the kitchen to bring vitality and imagination to the simplest arrangements. Jam jars, bottles, casserole dishes, earthenware jugs and shiny enamel pots—all can provide a natural setting for country flowers loosely and informally displayed. The hours that you spend in the kitchen, preparing meals and doing other tasks, can be made much more agreeable by having pleasant flowers around you. Arrangements of fresh herbs give a homey feel to the kitchen and are useful to have close by when you are cooking. Many herbs have unexpectedly attractive flowers, for example chives, sage, rosemary and thyme; others are perfect for leafy displays.

A RUSH BUTTER CONTAINER with its own gingham trimming is given over to sweetly scented daffodils, cut short and loosely bunched. A plastic yogurt carton serves as the inner container and the whole arrangement can be easily moved from shelf to breakfast table.

A KITCHEN WINDOWSILL comes alive with a bunch of daffodils, cut to different lengths and casually arranged in a pottery jug. With the leaves removed, varied shades from bright yellow to cream form a burst of living sunshine.

Smaller arrangements of assorted flowers and leaves share the windowsill, set informally in medicine bottles and a wine glass.

A *Brighter Breakfast*

A COLOUR THEME links the enameled coffee pot and its bright tulips, radiating sunshine from a corner into the kitchen. A single stem of prunus, placed at a jaunty angle, sets off the cheerful theme. Fresh herbs in glass jars provide a cool contrast and a subtle fragrance to the room.

OFFCUTS from a formal dining room arrangement have found their way to the breakfast table. Alstroemeria, daisies and a single tulip are bunched in a pottery jar to be enjoyed before the business of the day begins.

MEMENTOS of a stroll in the garden, a mixed bunch of hosta leaves, grasses, *Clematis tangutica* and hypericum are arranged informally in a glass flask filled with pebbles and set inside a Chinese bamboo steamer. The grasses burst from the neck of the flask and the different textures add interest to this casual design.

AN ART DECO sugar sifter is the home for a bunch of primroses set in a fan of their own leaves, guaranteed to brighten up any coffee break. The air of springtime is expanded with two sprays of delicate blossom set at an angle, to provide a surprise element in this simple design.

The Big Day

Celebrations—from weddings to Christmas dinner or a child's birthday party—call for something really special in the way of flower arrangements. They challenge you to summon up your ingenuity and imagination so that the decorations are the perfect complement to their setting. By planning an overall theme for the occasion, you can create the mood with flowers. This could be a colour link or a stylistic scheme or even an idea borrowed from a painting.

For an outdoor party, particularly something like a daytime wedding reception, try to devise a theme that links the party setting, be it patio or marquee, with the garden itself. Keep your floral decorations simple so that they seem to arise spontaneously, and place them at eye level, where they will create festive areas of colour and keep the design theme in focus.

The concept for an indoor party needs to be much bolder in order to transform a familiar domestic interior into the setting for a celebration. Weave a theme out of primary colours for a child's party, with bold bright flowers linked to balloons, paper napkins and plates. Recapture the leisurely Edwardian way of life for a dinner party. Set the table with your finest silver and glass, crisp white napkins, finger bowls in which a few blooms float on faintly lemon-scented water and, for a final gracious note, a floral gift at each place.

At Christmas time, bring a really festive air to the house with armfuls of ivy and pine heaped on the mantelpiece and twined around the bannisters. Place bare twigs among the greenery, sprayed with gold and silver paint, with pots of scarlet poinsettia and white cyclamen. Add candles of all shapes and sizes. When lit, their soft gleam will fill the room and their warmth will draw out the pungent scent of the pine needles.

By careful planning and establishing an overall design with meticulous attention to every detail of your scheme, you can make any "big day" more exciting and memorable.

BOTTICELLI'S *Primavera* inspired this wedding table. It is draped with a brocade cloth on which are pinned fresh posies. An outdoor setting for such an arrangement provides the bonus of natural light which throws the flowers into high relief and casts soft shadows over the table as the day wears on.

The flowers and foliage making up each posy are inserted into a florist's tube, tied with ribbon and then pinned to the cloth. As a final touch, unused flower heads and petals are strewn on the lawn nearby.

Pastoral Romance

ADD A CELEBRATORY TOUCH to special occasions by making flowers an integral part of the table setting. Here, a plain wooden candlestick is transformed. Wrap fresh moss, slightly moistened, around the candlestick. Then, working from the top, insert glossy laurel leaves all the way down, in a pattern of overlapping rings. This can be done a day or two in advance of the occasion and, on the morning, fresh flower heads tucked between the leaves.

MINIATURE POSIES swing like mobiles from the branches of a candelabra. The flowers are placed in water-filled glass vials. The informality of such a use of flowers creates an unusual contrast to the formality of antique silver.

A NAME CARD on a dinner table is given a special welcoming touch by the addition of an individual floral gift. A florist's tube, the type in which orchids are sold, is put to good use and keeps the flowers fresh until guests arrive.

A ROMANTIC TABLE, set outdoors, is edged with trailing ivy, then white roses are tucked between the leaves. Such a green and white theme makes a perfect stage for the wedding cake and a special feature for guests to admire during a summer wedding.

Other tables can be similarly decorated, each with a centerpiece, such as a pedestal bowl of lush strawberries, to enhance the garden theme.

Flowers can naturally be linked with the colour scheme chosen for a wedding. Green and white is especially fresh and the various tones of white, from warm to cool, are seen in a wide range of flowers, including lilies and gypsophila. Another advantage of such a scheme is that greenery and white flowers are available from florists all year round. Other pleasing colour combinations are in the yellow to apricot and pastel pink to mauve ranges. Consult the colour illustrations on p. 16 and *Favourite Flowers* list (p. 152) for inspiration and to check the availability of colour varieties.

A Bridal Pathway

INDIVIDUAL BOUQUETS adorn the staircase in the bride's home and make a beautiful pathway to greet her on this very special day. Bouquets have been made by members of the family and friends, and put together with loving care and attention. What better way to send off a bride and wish her well in her new life?

Once the colour theme has been established, an assortment of flowers is assembled in different shades and tints of the same colour. The staircase is measured to assess the number of arrangements needed and wet foam blocks are wrapped in tinfoil and wired, with loose ends left for attachment. A single bouquet is made to demonstrate the technique and the desired effect.

Working on a ladder, or on a chair placed on a table, facilitates the arranging of the bouquet *in situ*, with the foam block attached at eye level. When complete, each arrangement is linked with generous loops of wide satin ribbon, adding the finishing touch to this festive display.

The range and variety of each bouquet is of great interest to family and guests. At the end of the day, as a special gesture of thanks, each creator may be given an arrangement to take home as a reminder of the happy occasion.

Festive Mantelpieces

A CASCADE OF EVERGREEN foliage is taped to the marble mantel and the fixings are disguised with more branches, held in position with twists of florist's green wire. Spaces are left for candlesticks to be added on Christmas Eve.

This is the season of the year for celebration and generosity, and your flower displays should give forth the same air.

MATCHING MANTELPIECE arrangements at different levels link the Christmas theme. Candles are especially festive and a row along the mantelpiece, rising out of a bed of rich aromatic pine, creates a focus of attention. The branches seem almost to arrange themselves, falling in a natural tracery of movement.

POINSETTIA STEMS, cut from potted plants, appear to float above a collection of smooth white pebbles and are guarded on either side by highly polished candlesticks. Crammed together in a "non-arranged" way, the scarlet bracts form a rich cluster against the pale background. Several green leaves are left for contrast and, as a final touch, a few sprays of gypsophila add a stardust texture to the whole design.

The cut stems of poinsettia must be sealed before arranging, otherwise the milky sap will foul the water. Hold the cut ends in a flame for several seconds, which sears the tips (see p. 134).

Glass containers offer an ideal opportunity to dress the arrangement from within.

Smooth pebbles, seashells, crinkled aluminum foil, coloured marbles and, for the festive touch, Christmas tree baubles—all can be used to create that extra design feature in your arrangement.

Christmas Flowers

A GOOD-MORNING TRAY, set with heirloom china brought out for the annual festivities, sets the mood for family togetherness.

Foil-wrapped chocolate pennies and glittering miniature boxes and crackers are the first gifts of the day. The napkin is spangled with a spray of gypsophila to look like snowflakes.

A GAY RIBBON decorated with shiny baubles ties a napkin, from which a chocolate Santa Claus peeps out. The

buttonhole of baubles, heather and holly can later be pinned to the dressing gown or pullover in which you greet the family on Christmas morning.

RED IS A TRADITIONAL Christmas colour. Bunching about half a dozen red carnations tightly together into a single, big, fluffy flower head gives greater emphasis and a blaze of colour. A group of wine flasks with matching arrangements would make a fine display on a mantelpiece, hall or buffet table.

The red ribbon contributes to the design; gold, silver or tinsel ribbon could be chosen to match a wrapping-paper theme. The flowers are held in place with a wedge of moss and, as a final touch, a collar of bright green laurel leaves adorns the rim.

TINY NOSEGAYS decorate each place setting, to welcome guests to the table. Nosegays can be made in advance with evergreen foliage and holly berries, with flowers added at the last moment. Improvise and invent, using gift-wrapping materials to give a seasonal flavour.

A centerpiece of large poinsettia heads nestles in a shallow glass dish, the bracts dramatically silhouetted against the black lacquered tabletop in a bold splash of colour.

A VICTORIAN STYLE is given to these pretty nosegays surrounded by a lacy ruff made from a paper doily cut through to the center. The flowers and leaves are arranged in the hand and held securely with a rubber band, then slipped along the cut line to the middle, so that the doily wraps around them, the cut edges overlapping. The stems are trimmed afterward to the same length for a tailored finish. Alternatively, you can cut a small hole in the center of the doily, by folding it in half and then in half again.

Miniature gold balls add sparkle to the nosegays, and some foliage pirated from potted plants gives variety.

Party Tables

ROSEBUDS FOR A BRIDE'S dressing room overflow from a stencilled straw basket. The silver bowl alongside is heaped with shredded paper packing from chocolate boxes, colour-linked with the roses and cranberry glass to make a delicate table arrangement. The surprise is that the roses are made of marzipan, so that this edible flower feast can be shared with the wedding guests afterward.

FANCY DRESS COCKTAILS are the order of the day in the Caribbean and Far East where a visual kick is given to drinks by decorating them with tropical flowers—orchids, hibiscus and bougainvillea. To capture this gaiety, you don't need exotic flora—a bright red gladiolus head does the job just as well. Less showy but more flavoursome are sprigs of mint, twists of lemon or cucumber, and pineapple wedges. The simplest glass of mineral water benefits from this glamorous treatment.

A PARTY TABLE gets an instant new look with a can of spray-on colour and simple cut-out paper daisies. On a white paper tablecloth, dried, pressed fern leaves are laid in recurring patterns and sprayed with colour or glitter. The leaves are then taken away and a pale silhouette of each remains. The background takes on a soft shadowy effect, like a glade. The flowers are cut in a variety of shapes from folded paper and scattered among the food delicacies on the table.

BRIGHTEN-UP TABLECLOTHS with another idea of cut-out paper flowers from a seed catalog mixed in with decorative paper angels, bought from the gift-wrapping counter. All kinds of cut-out motifs can be used to suit the occasion. Link the colours of the motifs and tablecloth to achieve an effective scheme.

All the family can participate in making these decorations, a job which keeps them occupied while other important arrangements for food, flowers and seating are going on.

The Office

Most of today's offices are less formal than they were even ten years ago. The emphasis now is on a more youthful, relaxed and vital business image. Heavy, dark furniture, somber furnishings and dull upholstery have given way to lighter brighter colours and finishes. Even office equipment, such as filing cabinets and desk furniture, comes in a range of zingy colours—scarlet, bright green, yellow, blue. The transformation has been completed by the upsurge in the number of people who own home computers and have set up an office or "work station" in their own homes.

Potted plants and flowers in the office are no longer considered simply as "the feminine touch" or as a luxury. They are regarded as an important factor in the creation of a cheerful, bright working environment. They can highlight dull areas, create interest and bring a feeling of comfort and relaxation to workers that will be reflected in their output and their mental attitude.

When flowers are displayed in the office it is helpful to observe a few simple "rules." First, and most important, they should need minimal attention. Second, containers should have clean uncluttered lines and should be substantial enough not to be easily knocked over by the day-to-day passage of people. Another factor to consider is cost—no business can afford to renew great floral arrangements every other day. It therefore makes sense to buy flowers that are in season and that are robust and long-lasting. Various types of foliage can also be bought that are trouble-free and look good for days. Dried flower arrangements play an important part in the office too, since they can be taken out from time to time when fresh flowers are difficult to come by or are too expensive.

GOOD LIGHTING keeps an all-grey room from looking dull. The geometric shapes of the interior and furniture are softened by the curved branches of a tall evergreen plant, which gives an immediate warmth to the working atmosphere.

ARRANGEMENTS IN AN OFFICE should be inexpensive and trouble-free. This bowl of young eucalyptus foliage, set on a side table among toning objects, steals the limelight.

The matching vase and lamp base, and the sprays of foliage themselves, echo the swirling lines of the dove painting on the wall and the sculpture in front. The neutral scheme of various tones of grey, ranging from charcoal to the pale tint of morning mist on the walls, makes for a pleasing and peaceful atmosphere. The hint of green in the leaves and the strong areas of white lighten the scheme and relieve it from monotony.

The eucalyptus leaves will last for several weeks, and the arrangement can be varied from time to time by adding a single colourful bloom. The quiet understatement of such a display is perfect for a busy office and it retains its freshness with a minimum of time and effort.

Working Flowers

HALF A DOZEN TULIPS line up in a glass vase through which their stems and curling leaves can be seen. The playful nature of the group can be changed, by cutting the stems to different lengths or using more or fewer flowers to achieve a variety of effects.

Tulips continue to mature in water; their stems twist and change, buds open and full blooms reveal black stamens, adding fresh interest each day.

A WHITE VASE filled with a mass of white daisies set on a white table creates a powerful white-on-white-on-white designer concept. The flowers are available all year round from florists and the display is simplicity itself in terms of arrangement, time and image. Over a two-week period, the design will change as discoloured leaves are removed and stems are cut shorter to prolong the flowers' vase-life. The scale of the arrangement changes with a finale of domed daisy heads resting on the rim of the vase. A few pieces of charcoal will help to keep the water fresh.

Dried Flowers

Arranging dried plant material can be every bit as creative as arranging fresh flowers and a wide variety is available from florist and gift shops. All sorts of garden material can also be treated and used in light-hearted, inventive arrangements which can be added to frequently so they do not get tired-looking. Flower heads, petals, seed pods, plantains, leaves, grasses, even "weeds"—all these can be used to give endless scope and variety to dried displays. Pieces of driftwood, pebbles or shells can also be added.

Flowers dry out to muted hues and, as they grow older, take on a hint of soft beige. If an arrangement becomes too muted, rejuvenate it by adding a dash of fresh colour for accent or tucking in several younger dried flowers.

Large displays full of texture and softness are made by grouping together bunches of seed heads or grasses, all of the same species. When you collect wild grasses, pick them just before the seed heads are fully open and tie the bundles in handfuls with rubber bands. This makes them easier to manage afterward and the stems are less likely to bend or break when placed in position. Some flowers are grown for their seed heads alone, which make wonderful displays when clustered together.

MIXING artificial and fresh flowers creates an interesting effect. Starting with a dome of green and silver leaves, some fresh flowers are added and then an abundance of silk flowers. At a glance you cannot tell the real from the unreal. The foliage is long-lasting and the arrangement is renewed simply by adding new flowers.

A MISCELLANY of dried summer flowers placed in an antique china jug makes a lovely welcome, the seashells and stones complementing the colour scheme. You can add a touch of fragrance to this dried bouquet by spraying it with potpourri reviving essence, available from florists in a variety of scents.

Scaled to Size

A PERMANENT DISPLAY of dried material in a hall of natural wood and muted colours becomes a major decorative feature, almost a piece of furniture. Placed at the foot of the stairs, it can be viewed from all angles and reveals something new each time you look at it.

Such an arrangement can be constantly changed according to the setting and the availability of material. Naturally dried plants of all kinds form the basis, with a range of teazels and bunches of tall grasses combining to give a burst of earthy colours and textures. Translucent honesty provides the highlights and pheasants' feathers are added for variety of form.

At one time, giant banana leaves tumbled from the base of this arrangement, to be replaced later with more honesty which, when illuminated with uplighters, becomes a spectacular sight.

A MINIATURE STILL LIFE is created with a small vase of dried poppy heads, helichrysum and tiny flowers, set on a wicker chair and backed by a toning drape. The Chinese bowl with a chrysanthemum pattern completes the scheme.

With dried arrangements, you need not worry about spilling water or spoiling delicate textiles or antique furniture. You can also experiment with containers you would not normally use for flowers—baskets, unglazed terra-cotta, porous pottery, leaky metal containers and even cracked vases you don't want to throw away.

ARCHITECTURAL SIMPLICITY is achieved with a bunch of dried bamboo leaves rising out of a Keith Murray vase from Wedgwood. Dried anthurium stems project at an angle.

MAKING THE MOST OF FLOWERS

Your own style of flower design, developed through practice,
and inspired by the illustrations on the preceding pages,
is as personal as the decorative scheme in your own home.
It should complement and blend with your favourite possessions to make
a unique personal statement evocative of mood and season.

The reference section that follows offers all the basic
"know how" you need to choose and care for flowers and foliage,
and to translate your ideas into pleasing designs. By handling
flowers throughout the year you can learn techniques that
ensure maximum effect. The operations of choosing flowers and
containers, examining the textural and colour qualities of
plant material, placing arrangements against appropriate
backgrounds and lighting them imaginatively – all are part of
a learning process that combines many artistic sensibilities.

Cut flowers, and the designs of which they become a part,
are things of transience. But that very transience is one of
the special qualities of a flower arrangement. With careful
choice and treatment, in transporting them and arranging them at home,
flowers become living pictures. To extend the life of plant material,
it can be dried and preserved, or you can use
the best of modern artificial flowers for all or part of a design.
There is no end to the permutations and combinations available.

The mechanics of flower care and arrangement are the basis of success.
With practice, expertise will follow.
By using plant material as the artist selects colours from a palette,
you can extend your appreciation of colour and design into
your environment.

In the following pages, some traditional methods of flower arranging
are described along with the novel modern ideas
that form the basis of this book. To illustrate certain points
and to allow you to view the designs in a fresh light each time,
cross references are made to many of the pictures in the book.
The position of pictures on a page are abbreviated,
so that *t* means top, *b* bottom, *l* left, *r* right, *tl* top left, and *br* bottom right.

CHOOSING FLOWERS

The pleasure of giving and receiving flowers is lessened if blooms arrive in poor condition. So it is worthwhile taking a little trouble to make sure that they do not suffer in transit. Here are some hints to help you pick flowers, buy them and transport them so that they have the best chance of looking fresh on arrival.

PICKING GARDEN FLOWERS

Flowers from the garden are the freshest and most inexpensive of all the blooms available to the flower arranger. Pick them when the sun is not at its height and, to help prevent wilting, carry a bucket of tepid water around with you, recutting the stems under water as you go. After picking, leave the bucket in a cool dark place for several hours—preferably overnight—to allow the flowers to recover before you arrange them. Apply any special treatments to flowers or foliage as necessary (see p. 134).

When choosing plants for your garden, keep colour and texture in mind. Plan flowering periods so that some of your favourites are available throughout the year.

BUYING FROM FLORISTS

Flowers bought in season are at their best and cheapest; buy several bunches of the same colour to make a dramatic display. Whatever flowers you choose, check that the stems are strong and the foliage crisp and undamaged. Make sure the flowers are well wrapped by the florist. Keep these tips in mind when buying certain flowers:

CARNATIONS

split calyx

Choose good sturdy stems. Check that the center is not showing and watch out for a split calyx.

CHRYSANTHEMUMS: Fresh single varieties have firm green centers, with only a little pollen showing. Check the underside of double varieties for discoloration and loose petals.

DAFFODILS: Best chosen when the flowers are in loose bud, with leaves attached. Full blooms should have a crisp feel and no pollen evident.

TULIPS: Choose strong stems, spotless foliage and green-tinted buds. Watch out for weak floppy stems in pre-wrapped bunches.

HYDRANGEAS: Potted plants are a good buy because the flowers last well and, at the end of the season, dry on the plant to give heads of subtle hues, useful in dried arrangements.

FREESIAS

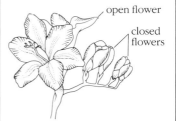

open flower

closed flowers

When buying, make sure that only the bottom flowers on the stem are open.

LILIES: Watch for broken stems and buds with a slightly transparent wrinkly look. Such buds may have been overchilled in transit and will never open fully. The same is true of cultivated iris, sold in tight bud in early spring.

ORCHIDS

florist's tube

Stems are sold in a florist's tube or moisture-holder filled with damp cotton balls. Orchids are hardy and long lasting, but check flowers for bruising and marked or missing lip-petals. Do not spray with water.

POPPIES: A good florist will have sealed the stems by burning the ends, for longer life. Buy in bud with just a little colour showing.

PYRETHRUM: Look for hard green centers, without much pollen.

ROSES: Buds should be firm but not too tight or they may never open. Flowers respond well to commercial preservatives, but see the Care Chart (p. 135) for special treatment.

ARTIFICIAL FLOWERS

Do not ignore the special qualities of artificial plant material: It is light, impervious to temperature extremes, easy to use and never wilts or dies. Arranged with fresh or preserved foliage, asparagus fern or gypsophila, paper or "silk" flowers look wonderful. Stridently green stems sometimes spoil the illusion in the cheaper polyester flowers, but these can be hidden within the arrangement or replaced by natural stalks. Plastic berries for Christmas decorations add a festive touch to glossy evergreens, and artificial flowers for parties can be arranged well in advance. Remember to disguise the mechanics of the arrangement by masking with pebbles, moss, glass fragments or small pieces of bark.

Plastic blooms set in a bold container offer possibilities of making your own witty design statement, linking a colour scheme or complementing a party theme. But take a fresh look at all artificial material, appreciate its special colour quality and use it with confidence. Seek inspiration from fine art—masters such as Chagall and Fantin-Latour depict flowers and their colours with a touch of magic.

Crystal or porcelain flowers, carved wooden fruit, blooms made up from feathers or dried natural material, such as fir cones, poppy seed heads and preserved leaves—all can be used with flair to make a grand gesture for the special occasion.

IN THE COUNTRY

Wild flowers can be kept fresh by putting them immediately into a plastic bag lined with wet paper or moss, then sealing the bag. But remember—never pick protected species of flower and never dig up their roots for your own garden.

Wild grasses, picked on a dry day and when their seed heads are full, can be successfully bunched to fill a basket or large bowl. Used directly as dried material, grasses give months of pleasure; added to fresh flowers, they give delicacy to an arrangement.

bunches of same colour, p. 22b, 43

carnations, p. 64tl

chrysan-themums, p. 43

daffodils, p. 107

tulips, p. 91

dried hydrangeas, p. 127

freesias, p. 76

lilies, p. 85

orchids, p. 95

roses, p. 13

silk and fresh flowers, p. 126

linking schemes, p. 67

feathers and dried ma-terials, p. 34b

fir cones, p. 116

wild grasses bunched, p. 78b

wild grasses with fresh flowers, p. 28tl, 51, 108b

FLOWERS ON THE MOVE

TRANSPORTING FLOWERS

damp paper

chicken wire

Car journeys, especially in hot weather, can be disastrous for cut flowers. A good way to prevent them fading is to condition them overnight in a bucket of cold water and pack them the next day. The best protection is to put the flowers in a cardboard box lined with plastic and padded with damp paper, then sealed with a lid. Flowers can also be kept in water on a long journey: A bucket, weighted with stones, half-filled with water and wedged securely in the car, ensures the flowers' fresh arrival. The bucket can be covered with chicken wire, its mesh providing support and protection for special or individual blooms. Flowers that bruise easily, such as camellias and lilies, can be put in separate glass jars and slotted into a bottle carrier or a compartmentalized wine basket.

Assemble your bouquet with crisp tissue and ribbon (the water-repellant kind is best) at the last parking place before your destination and present your hostess with beautiful fresh flowers.

HOSPITAL FLOWERS

Wards are hot, nurses overworked and tall stems get in the way. When choosing flowers for someone in hospital, a single exquisite bloom in a pretty container is a joy and easily accommodated on a bedside table. A small dried arrangement in a basket *(opposite, 1)* or a small bowl of potpourri petals *(2)* lasts well through convalescence and after. A posy of fresh flowers arranged in a container of wet foam *(3)* looks lovely.

Remember spring flowers last better in water than in foam.

Brightly coloured flowers (reds and yellows) are cheery for the convalescing patient, but can be an irritant to the very ill. Pastel shades are preferable. Avoid strongly scented flowers for the sick since these can be heady and cloying. Soft-smelling herbs, such as mint and lavender, are well worth considering.

You may like to write a short note about the flowers you bring. The language of flowers was a code understood in Victorian times when each type of bloom held a secret meaning. For example, an offering of moss, bearded crepsis, primroses, daisies and wood sorrel would have meant "May maternal love protect your early youth in innocence and joy." Choose your flowers for the special meaning they convey. Some charming messages are: Arum for ardour; forget-me-not for true love; purple lilac for first emotions of love; magnolia for love of nature; orange blossom for your purity equals your loveliness; sweet pea for delicate pleasures; red poppies for fantastic extravagance.

Even colour varieties of the same type of flower have different meanings. For example, red roses express love, but yellow blooms may suggest feelings of jealousy.

A BASKET OF FRUIT, decorated with fresh flowers, is especially welcome at the sickbed. Hardy individual blooms such as small single chrysanthemums look and last well, tucked into a basket of fruit or bunched to one side. One spray, the flowers cut short, is enough.

A BOTTLE OF CHAMPAGNE is a wonderfully cheery gift for someone who is convalescing. It can easily be decorated by tying a single bloom to the neck of the bottle with a double bow of satin ribbon *(below, 4)*. Single orchids, sold in spill-proof glass tubes, are simple to attach to a gift. A tiny bunch of miniature roses or a few pansies decorating a gift-wrapped book add a charming personal touch.

LONG-STAY PATIENTS may spend many hours alone and it is often difficult to choose a gift, both beautiful and stimulating, for someone who is perhaps too frail to read. Consider giving a seashell—a wonderful pleasure to look at and to hold. Over a series of visits, bring along other miniature items such as some beautifully marked smooth pebbles from the beach. A small dish filled with silver sand *(below, 5)* could provide a home for all these treasures, bringing an oasis of memories to the bedside.

Your nurseryman may be able to supply an airplant (of the *Tillandsia* genus, originally from Central and South America) mounted on a piece of coral or in a shell. These small plants need only a fine spray of rainwater each day during summer and once a week in winter. Well-established airplants will eventually flower. Alternatively, a small cactus in a pot does not need much attention.

bedside flowers, p. 99t

fruit basket and flowers, p. 49t

single bloom in glass vial, p. 112b

oasis of memories, p. 99b

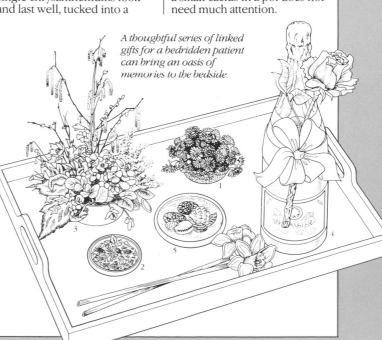

A thoughtful series of linked gifts for a bedridden patient can bring an oasis of memories to the bedside.

FLOWER CARE

Properly treated, fresh-cut flowers can last indoors for two to three weeks, or even longer. So it pays to take these few simple steps before arranging your flowers.

STEMS
As soon as possible after picking, recut stems under water and leave them submerged up to the flower heads for several hours, preferably overnight. When starting your arrangement (*below*), cut the stems

diagonally with a sharp knife (*1*) or secateurs (*2*). Do not just snap the stems by hand, since jagged tears can lead to infection. Next, remove all foliage that will be below water level (*3*). Woody stems should be split (*4*) or crushed with a hammer and the bottom 3 inches of bark removed from the ends.

FOLIAGE
The most convenient way to prepare leaves for decoration is to submerge them (with the exception of grey foliage) in the bath for several hours before use, preferably overnight. A spot of dishwashing liquid added to the water will remove any dust or city grime and give the leaves a glossy sheen.

BOILING WATER TREATMENT
Tender spring foliage, ferns and certain flowers (see Care Chart opposite) may need treatment with boiling water. It sounds drastic but works wonders.

Bring water to a boil in a wide saucepan (*below*). Protect flower heads and leaves with newspaper. Plunge 2 inches of stem ends into the boiling water, for about 5 seconds in the case of thin-stemmed flowers and not more than 30 seconds for thick stems. Hold the blooms at an angle to avoid steaming them. Place immediately in deep tepid water for a long drink. Stems may be recut later without further heat treatment.

SPRING FLOWERS
When using bulb flowers, such as daffodils or bluebells, cut into the green portion of the stem since the white part close to the bulb does not take up water satisfactorily.

Before arranging daffodils and other soft-stemmed spring flowers, recut the ends and soak overnight; this allows the sap to drain off. If arranged immediately after cutting, sap can foul the water and badly affect other flowers in the container.

Tulips, including foliage, may be wrapped in brown paper before immersing up to their necks in water. Some of the stems may twist after arranging, so symmetrical designs are not always easy to achieve. Tulips, in particular, seem to have a mind of their own.

SEARING
Poppies, euphorbias, zinnias and poinsettias need to have their stems sealed before arranging. Burn the cut ends in a flame for several seconds. Special care should be taken when removing poinsettia leaves to prevent excess weeping of the sap. The milky fluid from euphorbias can be an irritant to the skin and eyes.

FEEDING
Commercial preservatives are sometimes helpful in prolonging the life of cut flowers. Aspirin solutions, or even 7-Up, may also help (see Care Chart opposite). To make up such a preserving solution at home, mix together:
$1\frac{1}{4}$ cups of water
$\frac{1}{2}$ teaspoon sugar
$\frac{1}{2}$ teaspoon household bleach

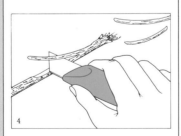

Soak flowers overnight in water, up to their necks. To keep tulip stems straight, wrap them in brown paper first and then soak.

FLOWER CARE CHART

For directions for searing, boiling water treatment and general flower care, see opposite

ANEMONES   Best in water, less happy in foam.

ANTIRRHINUMS   Garden varieties: Put in deep water for minimum of 4 hours before arranging. Slit woody stems. Nursery blooms that have been forced: Dip stem ends briefly in boiling water, then soak.

BAMBOO   Do not cut until late summer. Dip stem ends in boiling vinegar for 2 to 3 minutes. Tricky for the beginner since leaves are apt to curl, but worth experimentation if you have a supply.

CAMELLIAS and GARDENIAS   Bruise easily, so handle with care. Floated in shallow water, they make an unusual feature on a dining table. Glossy attractive leaves.

CARNATIONS   Garden "pinks" give the best scent. Greenhouse or imported varieties with woody stems: Split or crush ½ inch at ends and cut between joints with a slanting cut. Soak well before using in foam or arrange directly in slightly warm water. Respond well to 7-Up added to water.

CHRYSANTHEMUMS   Long-lasting and hardy. Remove foliage below waterline and check for freshness before buying (see p. 132). Cut above "heel," where stem joins main branch, since water will not be taken up if stem is broken off at joint.

CLEMATIS   Dip stem ends in boiling water for 30 seconds. Unreliable as cut flowers, but seed heads are wonderful for dried arrangements.

CROCUSES   Use in water for miniature arrangements. When bunching, do not use tight rubber bands which restrict take-up of water in soft stems; bind with wool instead. Autumn-flowering crocus (*Colchicum*) can be cut and arranged in same way, or will bloom indoors from bulbs set in a saucer of pebbles without water or soil.

DAHLIAS   Dip stem ends briefly in boiling water, then allow a long drink before arranging.

EUPHORBIAS and POINSETTIAS   Sear cut stems as directed on opposite page. Take care to wash milky sap off skin; it can cause irritation, especially if rubbed near eyes.

FERNS   Insert stem ends in boiling water for 30 seconds, then submerge for a long drink.

FORSYTHIA   Cut sprays when buds are tight, to bloom early indoors. Leave in warm water and watch flowers open.

GERBERA   Recut stems and place ends in boiling water for 20 seconds. If you require straight stems, suspend them in a bucket of water so that the cut ends do not touch the bottom; support flower heads with slotted card supports or tape strung across the rim. Soak well in cool water. Last well once conditioned.

GLADIOLI   Remove topmost bud for the complete opening of flowers.

HELLEBORE (Lenten rose, Christmas rose)   Treat stem ends in boiling water for 30 seconds immediately after cutting. Then place up to necks in warm water for several hours. Keep away from direct heat. Mature blooms last best when cut.

HYDRANGEA   Best after flower heads are mature and "papery" to the touch. Place flowers under water for several hours and crush stem ends before arranging. Spray bracts occasionally with water. Once mature, dries well for winter arrangements.

LILAC   Strip all leaves. Batter stem ends and soak in deep water overnight. Leaves may be included in separate sprays. Same treatment for *Philadelphus* (mock orange blossom).

LILIES   Never attempt to prize open delicate lily buds. Split stems and remove leaves at base. Take care not to brush pollen against clothing or upholstery—it marks. Water lilies can be floated in a shallow container and drops of warm melted wax at base of petals will set to keep flowers open.

LUPINS   After picking, fill the hollow stems with water, then plug with cotton balls. A syringe is useful for doing this. Do the same with delphiniums and other hollow-stemmed flowers.

MIMOSA   Once fluffy stage is reached, flowers are fully mature and showing maximum pollen, so indoor arrangements are short-lived. Responds well to commercial fixing solutions but is best in moist conditions, arranged in very warm water for example. Once flower balls are spent, keep for dried arrangements.

ROSES   Garden varieties: Remove thorns and give deep-water treatment up to the flower heads before arranging. Florist's blooms: Recut stems and crush ends, wrap in stiff paper and give long drink in warm water. Any limp blooms can be placed in 4 inches of water, hot to the touch, for up to 15 minutes, then laid lengthwise in shallow water until revived. If buds are too tight when purchased they may never open fully, but strong stems are a good guide to quality. Roses respond well to commercial preservatives or one aspirin tablet to about 1 quart of water.

SPRING FLOWERS   Daffodils are best arranged apart from other flowers. Spring flowers prefer water, not foam. They respond well to a long drink before arranging in shallow water.

VIOLETS   Revel in moist conditions and best arranged close together in small groups. Spray well with water and keep cool. Wilting cut flowers can be totally immersed until revived. Note African violets (*Saintpaulia*) must not be submerged and take care when watering not to splash the leaves.

glass cylinders
with stems,
p. 28 tr, 63, 75

glass cubes
with pebbles,
p. 87b

cylinder with
stones and
shells, p. 102 tr

shelf group-
ings, p. 89

dinner place-
ments with
bottles
pp. 40–41

different
bottle shapes,
p. 64r

vases in
graphic pairs,
p. 71

integrated
designs, p. 19,
78t

visual links,
p. 47, 66

black vases,
p. 42, 89

cookie sheets,
pp. 38–39

roasting pan,
p. 21

serving tray,
p. 41 tl

liqueur glas-
ses and cups,
p. 88r

plastic bottles,
p. 51

baskets, p.
22t, 36–37

hollowed-out
fruits, p. 38 tl

jelly molds,
p. 90t

milk bottles,
p. 85

ashtrays,
p. 38b

CHOOSING CONTAINERS

Over the years, any flower arranger builds up a collection of containers and vases, although some will prove more useful than others. If you are starting from scratch, consider a basic collection of vases that ranges from the tall and narrow cylindrical glass types to shallow ceramic dishes, together with an assortment of specimen vases and bottles for early or late season single blooms and small flowers.

Plain undecorated vases seem to work well in most settings. They are "safe." Glass cylinders or cubes are particularly useful since the crossed patterns of the stems extend the visual link right up to the flower heads. Pebbles or small stones used underwater as stem supports look decorative when seen through a plain glass container.

When buying a specimen vase or small container, invest in six or more of the same kind. You can then set up individual dinner placements or a variety of table or shelf groupings to achieve special effects. Alternatively, for a more casual and less expensive approach, start collecting bottles of more or less the same size; different shapes can add an attractive feature.

For a graphic approach, consider at least one pair of larger vases displayed at either end of a serving table or mantelpiece, or even side by side. A personal choice of vase for such arrangements would be the modern rectangular glass type or white glazed pottery.

If for some reason you need to keep your range of vases to a minimum, think of other bowls or containers that can double up for flower arrangements. Buy only a few good basics and consider carefully the shape, size, texture and colour.

The vases that are suggested here are standard items in most china and glass stores and look good in any style of room setting, whether modern or traditional: A pair of rectangular glass vases, 6 × 9 inches; 6 small specimen glass vases; a cylindrical container, 6–9 inches; and a low wide bowl that can double as a salad bowl.

A container should be seen as an integral part of a design, tablescape or room setting. Although flowers are beautiful in themselves, the right vase can significantly enhance the mood of any arrangement. Consider, for example, how natural and "country" summer roses look in an earthenware jug; compare the same roses in an elegant silver urn or crystal bowl, gracing a formal dinner table. Although very different,

both are right. The lesson—dress the flowers appropriately for the occasion or situation, as you would dress yourself.

Plan the effect you wish to create—the tactile link of foliage to container, the colour link of flowers to other objects besides the immediate colour link or contrast of the vase. The spirit of your design will be enhanced by linking the plants with the container; for example, pastel blooms look best in gently coloured glazed china, fostering a romantic look. Black is a contemporary designer colour for vases, especially valuable for its dramatic impact when used with striking plant material, interesting textures and bold primary colours.

UNCONVENTIONAL CONTAINERS: As well as the usual simple and novelty containers for flowers, the kitchen or larder is a wonderful source of container surprises, for example, baking trays and pans, salad bowls, serving trays, liqueur glasses, tumblers, plastic bottles, baskets and even hollowed-out vegetables or fruits. Here are some points to consider when choosing and caring for your containers.

A collection of unconventional containers could include (1) horseshoe cake pan; (2) novelty eggcup; (3) empty sardine can; (4) sauté pan; (5) brioche pan; (6) wine bottle; (7) bread crock; (8) heart-shaped cake pan; (9) ramekin; (10) plastic ice cream container; (11) a rack of test tubes.

Choosing Containers

GLASS

Keep glass scrupulously clean and never allow foliage below the waterline since this quickly makes the water murky. Watermarks can be rubbed away with a wedge of lemon dipped in salt. Slime and dirt are best removed from tall narrow vases by adding a little concentrated dishwasher powder to the water and leaving it overnight. Chicken wire and foam are not suitable in glass containers—the wire can scratch the glass or stain it with rust marks, and foam is difficult to disguise or hide. Stems are best anchored in pebbles, sand, marbles or chunks of glass.

Take a new look at everyday items such as wine bottles, make-up jars, perfume bottles; they can contribute to a fascinating decorative scheme when used imaginatively.

POTTERY AND PORCELAIN

Simple, undecorated plain-coloured vases are always easy on the eye; decorated or highly patterned containers are more difficult to use since their extra decorative element must be taken into consideration in the overall design.

Garden flowers loosely bunched in an old blue and white stenciled jug will brighten any room. Link pastel-coloured glazed china to pretty flowers, natural pottery glazes to more earthy colours and grasses. Kitchen bowls or casserole dishes used with foam are excellent standbys for special occasions or extra-large quantities of flowers.

CRAFT POTTERY

Original artist-designed craft vases and pottery modeled by children are unique and provide a challenge for theatrical effect. Studio pottery and glass, design features in their own right, reveal their beauty anew when adorned with flowers and foliage. Draw attention to the artistry of a

A collection of conventional containers might include glass cylinders, cubes, glazed pottery, baskets, specimen vases and urns.

valuable vase by choosing plant material that will enhance its line, texture and colour. If you are anxious about water absorption or possible damage, insert a plastic or metal inner container; for regular use, a custom-made receptacle is invaluable. The Picasso vase has its own inner container, made to measure.

SILVER

Most flowers take on a special quality against silver's reflective surface. Silver is formal on a mantelpiece or dinner table, romantic on a dressing table. Tall flowing arrangements, grouped in foam and trailing over candlecup holders, are the traditional stock-in-trade of the flower artist. But for variation, try using candlesticks as witty conversation pieces by decorating them with flowers.

Since water and flower stems can mark silver, careful protection and cleaning are essential. Rinse and dry before use. Plastic-coated wire netting will not scratch. Metal pinholders must, however, be used with discretion, especially in antique items.

PEWTER

Pinks and mauves and other soft pastel shades complement pewter—grey foliage is especially attractive. Flowers floating in shallow water on a pewter plate feature happily on the dinner table.

METAL

Bronze, copper and brass must be checked for leaks; if in doubt use a glass or plastic inner container. Cleaning can be a chore, but the "long life" polishing agents are helpful and a mixture of lemon and salt, or vinegar and salt, will remove any stubborn stains. Rinse well before use. With antique urns, check the tap outlet carefully for leaks and incorporate the lid in the tablescape design.

Link the colour of flowers and foliage with the metal container. Brass and bronze look well with yellow and gold flowers; copper is enhanced by autumn tints, also rich burgundies and mauves. Dried grasses and foliage treated with glycerine are great with copper and brass.

ALABASTER

It is best to insert an inner glass or plastic bowl, wedged with moss to ensure it remains firm. Keep alabaster away from direct heat, which will spoil its structure, and wipe with olive oil from time to time.

MARBLE

Although marble is more hard-wearing than alabaster, special care is needed when using antiques. Plastic-coated wire will not scratch or stain. Pale or dark marbles look equally good, enhancing exotic arrangements or large groupings of flowers or foliage in a natural tumbled way.

anchoring stems among pebbles, p. 87b

in sand, p. 102r

among marbles, p. 98

among chunks of glass, p. 65

glazed china, p. 78

earthenware pots, p. 22b, 31

kitchenware, p. 90t

pottery made by children, p. 80r

studio pottery, p. 78, 82–83

enhancing vase and flowers, p. 74l, 105

Picasso vase, p. 80l

romantic silver, p. 95

Art Deco silver, p. 109

silver candlesticks, p. 112tr

linking flowers and metal containers, p. 44

copper container, p. 91

using marble, p. 53

*flowers in bas-
kets, p. 29,
34b, 37, 121t*

*bamboo con-
tainers, p. 46*

*carved
wooden
figures, p. 81*

*plastic con-
tainers, p. 51*

*weighting
with shells
and sand,
p. 102r*

*weighting
with pebbles,
p. 103b*

*novelty shell
treatments,
p. 99*

*decorative
shells, p. 102r*

*shells in their
own right,
p. 30, 127*

*hollowed-out
apples, p. 38*

*cookie sheet
and pudding
molds, p. 39*

*jelly molds,
p. 90*

*painting on
glass, p. 50*

CHOOSING CONTAINERS

BASKETS

All flowers, but especially unsophisticated arrangements of spring blossoms, look wonderful in baskets. Big baskets can be placed on the floor, while small ones are ideal on tables and dressers. Put a bowl inside the basket and pack it around with moss or crushed paper to prevent wobble. Fresh hanging-basket arrangements are best with foam, for graceful trailing effects; for lightness, dried or preserved material set in dry foam is ideal.

WOOD

Tea caddies, writing boxes, salad bowls and even pieces of driftwood (see p. 146) provide a charming foil for flowers. Remember to protect the wood from direct contact with water. Use a secondary container (a plastic mousse or yogurt carton will do) wedged firmly and disguised with moss or flowing plant material.

PLASTICS

Brightly coloured plastics are good for parties or outdoor jollities where breakages may be a problem. Plastic detergent or bleach containers come in wonderful colours. They can be cut to size with a sharp handy knife *(above)*. For special effects, you can spray them with glitter. Lightweight plastic may need weighting with pebbles or sand to prevent top-heaviness when the flowers are in place. Cast a fresh eye around your kitchen or bathroom—you may find some unconventional containers and accessories for flower arrangements.

SHELLS

Novelty treatments and surrealist ideas are fun to try out for special situations, but do not use shells in this way on a regular basis. They are best treated as you would flowers— as an arrangement in their own right.

FRUIT AND VEGETABLES

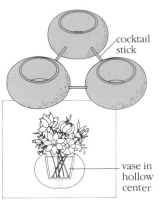

cocktail stick

vase in hollow center

Hollowed out, these make fun containers, with plastic or glass inserted to hold the water and flowers. Large exotic designs can be displayed in melons or pumpkins. When using small fruits, such as apples or oranges, anchor them so they will not roll away from your "still life;" simply spike them together with cocktail sticks *(above)*. Mounted on wooden meat skewers, small fruits can be incorporated into the heart of a flower arrangement.

CANS

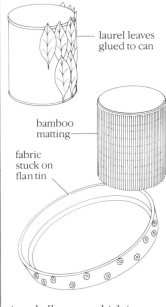

laurel leaves glued to can

bamboo matting

fabric stuck on flan tin

Any shallow can which is waterproof (such as an empty food can) is adaptable for

flower arrangements. Empty ham or fish cans, with the rough edges smoothed down, can be painted, covered over with hessian or string for a textured look, or even with leaves *(below, center)*. Baking trays, muffin pans or small pudding molds from the kitchen make unusual containers for table décor. When using foam, remember not to overfill the container since the water should occupy at least one-third of it—too much foam and it is impossible to top-up.

STORAGE

It is advisable to set aside a special cupboard where you can store your containers once you have washed and cleaned them thoroughly. Do not leave an empty container around as everyday decoration (unless of course it is a valuable piece of craft pottery) since this lessens its impact and enjoyment when it is used in a flower arrangement.

PAINT A GLASS JAR

There are many interestingly shaped glass jars which make good containers for informal flower displays. Don't throw old glass jars away; clean them out and remove the labels by soaking in water. Then decorate them by painting on flowers, faces, abstract designs; any number of motifs can be thought of and it is great fun for all the family. Use an oil-based gloss paint or enamel paints, which come in many colours, to protect your work from water. Alternatively, you can buy sticky labels or transfers in different shapes and colours and stick these on the jars.

WORKING MECHANICS

The basic equipment you will need for the mechanics of flower arranging is illustrated here. Try to keep your tools sharp and clean, and preferably all together in a basket or cardboard box. Make this "off limits" to the family so that items will not be missing or damaged when you need them.

It is useful when working with flowers *in situ* to have a large sheet of plastic on the floor to protect your carpet. Cuttings and general bits and pieces can be easily gathered up afterward and the plastic wiped dry to use again.

FLORIST'S FOAM

foam

This is sold in blocks or small cylindrical shapes, green for fresh arrangements and brown for dry ones. Submerge the green foam in warm or cold water—since different brands require different treatments, ask your florist's advice. A complete block will take at least 20 minutes to soak right through and needs to be weighted at first or it will float (a scale weight is ideal). When thoroughly wet, seal any unused pieces in a plastic bag since the foam will be unusable once it dries out.

Cut the foam to size, checking it is not dry in the middle. Place in the container and remember to leave at least one-third empty for the water to be topped up. Foam is useful in designs that demand trailing stems, as in mass arrangements, and for this reason it must extend well above the rim of the container. The cutaway diagram *(left)* shows how to prepare a large display in a deep bowl. Topping up with water every day is vital since the foam must not be allowed to dry out.

Polystyrene foam (the brown kind) is used in arrangements of preserved or artificial plant material. It can be used over and over again; sliced to shape, it needs no wrapping for use in swags. Since it is featherweight, dry foam is particularly useful for hanging arrangements.

PINHOLDERS

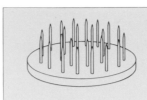

A pinholder, or "kenzan," is a small, relatively heavy, metal device consisting of regularly spaced sharp nails on which stems can be impaled *(above)*. Kenzans are extensively used in Japanese flower art in which branches are arranged at different angles in shallow dishes. The perfectionist may disguise the pinholder with pebbles or moss once the arrangement is complete. The beginner will find it helpful to secure the pinholder in the container with modeling clay or florist's fixative (which is not a glue, will not spoil the container and remains firm even under water).

Another type of pinholder has its own bonded container. Called a well pinholder, it is ideal for display with a group of curios or driftwood.

Using pinholders for stem support needs a little practice, but this technique is particularly useful for displaying sprays of blossom in shallow containers. Foam can also be impaled on the pinholder, but it tends to clog the pins. Pinholders are therefore usually used with water alone or to provide additional support with chicken wire inside a bowl.

trailing garlands arranged in foam, pp. 114–115

The equipment you will need for flower arranging consists of a sharp knife, wirecutters and secateurs (1); alternatively florist's scissors with a wire-cutting notch (2); a deep bucket (3)—plastic is best, it does not rust; squares of wide-mesh chicken wire with edges trimmed to leave ends that can be hooked around container rim (4); plastic-coated wire netting (5); watering can with fine spout for topping up (6); water spray to freshen flowers and foliage with a fine mist (7); transparent tape (8); gardener's green string (9) or raffia; rubber bands of various sizes (10); reel of rose wire (11) and florist's stub wires; florist's fixative, Blu-Tack or modeling clay (12); cocktail sticks for securing fruits in arrangements and for piercing plastic for garlands (13); cloth for mopping up (14); cooking oil which, used sparingly on a moistened cotton ball, will clean and polish leaves (15); pebbles, marbles, glass chunks or fine gravel for weight and décor (16); florist's moss or reindeer moss (17).

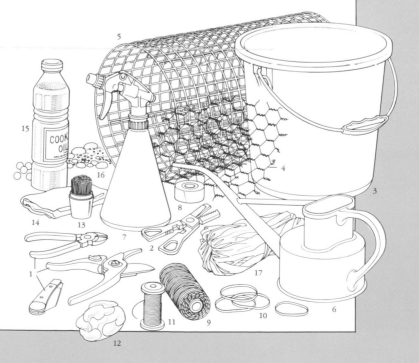

WORKING MECHANICS

*disguising the
mechanics
with moss,
p. 29*

*stem support
among peb-
bles, p. 87b*

*among glass
fragments,
p. 65*

*decorating
with pebbles,
p. 102r, 117*

*bunching
with green
string,
p. 118b*

*decorative use
of raffia, p. 81*

*woody
arrangement,
p. 34b*

*candles and
foliage,
p. 116*

*decorative
candlesticks,
p. 112*

CHICKEN WIRE

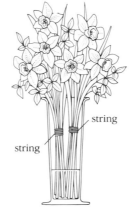

rubber band secures chicken wire

This type of wire mesh is indispensable for supporting stems inside containers and for easy transport of flowers. Keep a supply of ready-cut 12-inch squares of the wide mesh kind, wiping and drying them after use to prevent rusting. It is also possible to buy plastic-coated mesh that will not rust or scratch containers.

When gathering flowers from the garden, secure some chicken wire across the top of your water-filled bucket and slot the stems in as you go. This eliminates bruising or damage to the flowers later.

For arranging in foam, chicken wire can be draped over the foam block and then secured around the container with rubber bands, allowing the wire to hang down over the sides *(above)*. Used in this way for large arrangements, the wire gives additional support to thick stems that might otherwise cause the foam to crumble.

A square of chicken wire can be rolled into a loose ball and firmly attached to the container, by tying florist's wire all around it, like a parcel. The wire gives support without the use of florist's foam and is particularly helpful when arranging spring flowers or sprays of blossom, which last longer when placed directly in water. For heavy branches, you may find it useful to secure a pinholder at the bottom of the container with florist's fixative. Always disguise the wire with moss or foliage when the arrangement is complete.

PEBBLES, SAND AND GRAVEL

These can be used in a container to counterbalance heavy plant material. Glass chunks, seaglass or windshield fragments are attractive in transparent containers and also helpful in supporting stems with artistic effect. Sand or gravel can be used in the same way inside pottery but this can be difficult to keep absolutely clean.

Besides being attractive, pebbles are effective in disguising the mechanics of an arrangement. Collect round pebbles from the seashore in various colours. The broken pieces that have been smoothed and frosted by the waves are called seaglass and are found on beaches everywhere. Flat black stones can be found in many river beds and more rugged bits of rock or slate can be picked up on country walks. Develop a "seeing eye" for attractive pebbles and shells, and use them to complement or contrast with your plant material.

GARDENER'S GREEN STRING

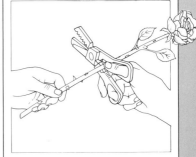

string

string

Use green string to bunch stems for placing within an arrangement. Bunching often gives more impact in a design than dotting individual blooms throughout. Natural coloured raffia can be similarly used for dried stalks and grasses.

RUBBER BANDS

As an alternative to string or raffia, you can use rubber bands for bunching, but be careful not to wrap them too tightly around soft stems. Rubber bands are also helpful when attaching chicken wire to a container: Put two thick bands right around the rim to ensure your mechanics are safe.

DRIFTWOOD

You can find interesting pieces of dead wood in rivers, streams, woodland and on the seashore. Sculptural pieces that have been thoroughly prepared (see p. 146) can add drama to a stark arrangement, enhance a woodland effect, make useful accessories and even hide the mechanics of an arrangement.

CONES

Green plastic cones, mounted on square sticks with wire or adhesive tape, are used to raise the height of material in a mass arrangement. Similar use can be made of yogurt pots, metal cigar containers or glass vials, filled with water or foam and mounted on sticks.

CANDLE FIXINGS

Candles to be featured within a design can be arranged in foam by inserting a few cocktail sticks into the base of the candle and pushing them into the foam. This keeps the candles steady and is less obtrusive than a plastic holder. The melted wax simply disappears into the container. In large arrangements, make sure that candle wicks are well clear of foliage since candles burn quickly and it is all too easy for such an arrangement to smoulder.

Candlecups, available from florists in both silver and brass, are small metal or plastic containers designed to fit inside candlesticks or narrow-necked bottles or vases. Fix firmly with florist's fixative. A universal fixing can be screwed into a bottle cork which is then cut to size for a tight fit.

THORN STRIPPER

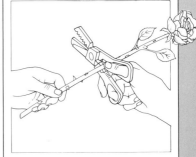

A florist's scissors with a wire-cutting notch can be used to strip bark from woody stems by gripping the bottom 2 inches of twig and pulling down. It can also be used for stripping thorns from roses, although a sharp knife is just as effective.

TECHNIQUES OF FLORAL DESIGN

The flower designs illustrated in this book are easy to adapt for your own home. Some of the following tips may be useful when trying out similar arrangements for yourself.

ARRANGING A SINGLE STEM

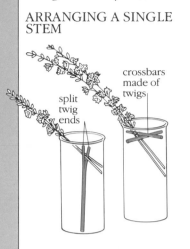

split twig ends

crossbars made of twigs

Besides placing a single stem in a narrow-necked vase or bottle, there are some delightful Japanese methods of flower art (called "ikebana") for securing single stems or a branch at an angle *(above)*. One method is to cut a twig a little shorter than the height of the vase and split its end, so it is fork-shaped. It rests against the inside of the vase. Then the branch to be displayed, its end also split, is placed in the fork and interlocked at the chosen angle. Alternatively, you can make an X-shaped fixing by crossing two small twigs and binding them with raffia, to form a support about 1 inch down the neck of the vase. The spray of blossom is then threaded between the crossbars.

Spring branches, no thicker than your little finger, can be gently bent into an artistic curve by pressing firmly between both hands. Thicker branches can be nicked and then bent slightly.

Pinholders are extremely useful, especially in shallow containers: Impale the branch straight on the pins and then slant it at the desired angle. Very thin stems can be bound together to fit firmly onto a pinholder or taped to 2 inches of a thicker stem to stand in the chosen position.

The simplest method of stem support, and one that is good since it is invisible with glass vases, is to run strips of transparent adhesive tape across the top of the vase and slot the stems in between them. Another idea is to place pebbles or glass fragments inside the vase and wedge the stems among them to provide support.

A more unusual method which looks a little oriental is to link three bamboo canes with shorter canes or small sticks, tying all together with raffia to form a stable tripod. Place the support outside the container and arrange your flower stem within this natural "cage." A variation on this theme, inspired by the supports given to herbaceous plants in the garden, is to rest a single stem against a bare twig or thread it through a maze of delicate twigs.

BUNCHING

A technique well worth perfecting is bunching in the hand for placing directly in a vase. To do this *(below)*, sort out your flowers by species and colour *(1)*. Bunch them loosely in the hand, testing for colour and proportions *(2)*. Check the stem length of the bunches against the height of the vase *(3)*. You can secure each bunch with a loose rubber band or with green string *(4)*. Then place the bunches directly in the vase and gently reshuffle them into a natural position *(5)*.

TUSSIE MUSSIE

This is an old-fashioned term for a nosegay—a welcome gift since it is usually made with a variety of sweet-smelling seasonal flowers. A tussie mussie is especially attractive with miniature daffodils, snowdrops, tiny roses and violets, complemented with dainty foliage such as rue, sprigs of rosemary or scented geranium leaves. Loosely bunched, ready to slip straight into a vase, it is charming presented as a Victorian posy. A florist can supply a posy frill for the professional touch.

single branch set at angle, p. 35, 92, 108–109

bunching flowers, p. 18tl, 66tr, 108b

Victorian posies, p. 119

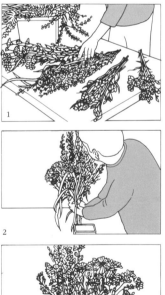

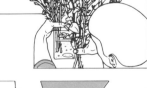

topiary art,
p. 31

baking tin
with moss,
p. 21

geometric
designs, p. 43

floral gifts,
p. 112b, 119

table settings,
p. 40

decorating
with ribbons,
pp. 118–119

flower basket
with moss,
pp. 36–37

TECHNIQUES OF FLORAL DESIGN

BUILDING STRUCTURES

chicken wire
with foam
wedged in

trunk
set in
plaster

A natural tree shape can be created by using a branch of silver birch as a trunk, set firmly in plaster inside a tub. Drape chicken wire over the trunk to the desired shape and wedge pieces of soaked florist's foam between the wire and trunk. Using stems of different lengths, place your flowers or foliage into the foam, disguising the wire with moss. Water-filled glass vials with single stems or branches can also be arranged within the framework. The diagram above shows such a structure, half-completed.

Miniature topiary trees can be features in party décor. Set in moss or foam, each in its own pottery tub, they can be decorated with berries, small rose hips or flower buds and daisies. For a fresh and modern look, consider making natural tree shapes, inspired by the umbrella tree, rather than the stylized cone shape typical of topiary art and the one usually seen in decorative floral schemes.

To create such an arrangement, invert a small pottery container over soaked foam, cut into a cylindrical block. Turn the container the right way up and use a knife to shape the foam. The foam is then used as a base on which to set the foliage. A skewer is useful to make a hole for each stem. Lightly spray the completed arrangement and leave it in a cool dark place until setting the table.

For the table, a square baking tray filled with damp moss or shallow pieces of foam forms the basis of a pattern depicted with short-stemmed flowers and foliage such as edging box (*Buxus suffruticosa*). For a buffet table, a national flag could be depicted or a heart shape for St. Valentine's Day. A pattern of plant material forming a geometric design, similar to the formal 'knot garden' of Tudor times, is attractive.

If you adapt cake-decorating themes to flower designs, a multitude of patterns is at your fingertips. For the special occasion, a design of individual table settings adds a personal touch. Arrangements of this kind can also be made in dried material, with coloured ribbons for decoration. Sketch out your design and choose colourful plant material that has been well conditioned beforehand.

A shallow dish or basket, lined with plastic and filled with moss, makes an ideal container for the first precious flowers of spring. Snowdrops or bunches of crocus are charming arranged in this way. You can also place the flowers in small water-filled jars or vials pushed into the mossy bed.

A tray lined with moss or florist's foam can be used to display a soft pyramid of flowers. Different varieties and colours are bunched at random, bringing to mind a miniature herbaceous border in a summer garden.

GARLANDS

Garlands are a classical form of floral design, especially suitable for such festivities as weddings and Christmas. Masters of woodcarving, such as Grinling Gibbons, are the inspiration for this graceful style, as are the intricate garlands that decorate the bowls and urns of Ancient Greece.

MAKING GARLANDS

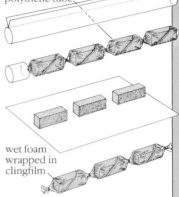

wet foam in
polythene tube

wet foam
wrapped in
clingfilm

For fresh garlands intended to swag a mirror or staircase and to last several days, you will need to use small pieces of wet foam encased in polythene tubing or clingfilm and secured at regular intervals like a string of square sausages *(above)*. Garlands can be heavy so it is wise not to be over-lavish with flowers and to make your foam packets no longer than 75 mm (3 in). Experiment with flat garlands laid on a buffet table and this will give you an idea of the amount of work and material involved. Remember

A string of foam squares, encased in polythene or clingfilm, forms the basis for the garland, shown half completed. Strong thread tied to the ends attaches it and the finishing touches should be made to the garland in situ.

TECHNIQUES OF FLORAL DESIGN

yogurt
pot

*staircase
garlands,
pp. 114–115*

*table décor,
p. 111, 113*

also that garlands rotate with the weight of material and so they must be delicately balanced and finished *in situ*. A graceful appearance is achieved by grading the size of flowers and limiting their numbers.

A less baroque effect can be achieved by looping ribbon between fresh arrangements, made up in foam-filled plastic containers or water-filled plastic pots, and then taping these to the stair rails *(above)*. Make sure that your fixings are ultra-safe since stairway garlands are often knocked aside. For a delicate effect, and one requiring fewer flowers, stems can be placed in florist's glass tubes and taped to woodwork.

This style is easily adapted for table décor or to looping around pillars, but the bunches of flowers must be dainty or the effect is spoiled. Glass tubes or metal tubes for cigars can be used to support flowers attached to a mirror or pinboard, or to form simple hanging arrangements.

DECORATING PEW ENDS

To make a beautiful path for the bride on her wedding day and give a celebratory air to the church or reception area, decorate the end of every third or fourth pew or row of chairs with a posy *(below)*, or a trailing arrangement on a pedestal. Alternatively, a pair of larger arrangements near the front is welcoming. Graded shades, of orange through apricot to yellow for example, with trailing ribbons in the chosen colour scheme lend a romantic touch.

Arrangements of silk or preserved flowers can be made up well in advance, using dry foam blocks, about 75 mm (3 in) square. Thread these with stub wires, leaving loops at either end for attaching the ribbon. No chicken wire or plastic seal is needed for dry arrangements since they are so lightweight. Insert the flowers and leaves in a pincushion fashion and attach the whole arrangement with florist's tape or ribbon.

Occasionally, church pews have permanent nail fixings for decorations, but if not, *do not* use drawing pins or damage the woodwork in any way.

HANGING ARRANGEMENTS

Using the same method as shown on p. 142, you can make hanging arrangements with fresh flowers using wet foam sealed in polythene film and covered with 15 mm (½ in) wire mesh. Such arrangements are particularly attractive hanging in marquees: they do not take up space and the flowers can be appreciated from below.

You can also use plastic spray-holders from the florist. These are easy to use and have handles with a hole for threading wire or ribbon. Make up with pre-soaked foam sealed with clingfilm and taped to the spray-holder. Since these plastic holders are larger than those generally used for such decorations, you may decide that one pair of arrangements for the principal setting is sufficient.

When making hanging arrangements or decorating pew ends, do not pierce the polythene packet from below or the water will leak out. All material used in garlands must be well conditioned in the usual way and it will benefit from a light spray of water as a final touch.

Attach arrangements to pew ends by looping ribbon over the pew edge and through the carved motif, letting the flowers hang about halfway down, with ribbon ends trailing. The first arrangement is made in a plastic cup filled with pieces of wet foam. The second is a posy made up in a block of foam and surrounded by a lacy doily.

*dried
arrangements,
p. 127,
128–129*

*soft effects with
gypsophila,
p. 65, 72*

*grasses with
flowers,
p. 28tl, 51,
108b*

*frosted fruits,
p. 57*

DRYING AND PRESERVING

The soft colouring of dried grasses, seed heads and preserved leaves brings warmth and texture to a room. Dried arrangements are especially welcoming in a vacation home which is often empty for long periods.

Preserved flowers and foliage play an ever-increasing role in the decorative schemes of busy people. Besides their aesthetic qualities, they are extremely practical and relatively inexpensive. Dried flowers make welcome gifts and travel well. They are available in a huge variety of colours, which you can arrange yourself or personalize an arrangement bought direct from the florist. Grasses and small flowers, such as London pride (*Saxifraga umbrosa*) and gypsophila, can look insignificant when arranged individually, but bunched collectively they create a soft cloud effect and add a new component to the overall design.

Arrange your dried materials in the brown foam, which is available from florists, weighted down on a heavy pinholder. Keep dried arrangements dust-free (a hairdryer is useful here) and looking fresh. Artificial flowers and plastic berries can be added to give a touch of colour that is sometimes lacking. Spraying and gilding can achieve spectacular results and glitter is fun to add at party time. Preserved foliage such as grasses and seed heads can also be used with fresh flowers to add a light touch, but remember to dry off the stems after use.

Fresh grapes, cherries and small fruits can be "frosted" by dipping them in egg white and then confectioners' sugar for table decoration. Crystallized flowers add a delicate touch to a dessert tray; violets, for example, are both pretty and edible.

PRESERVING PLANT MATERIAL

Most plant material can be preserved with ease. There are three basic methods: Air drying, preserving with glycerine or desiccants, and pressing. You can also do interesting things by bleaching wood and skeletonizing leaves.

AIR DRYING

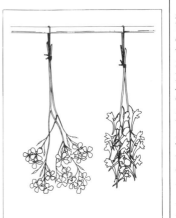

When the weather is dry, pick perfect specimens only. Harvest grasses and seed heads when they are fully ripe. Gather your material into small bundles, tie with wool and hang upside-down *(above)* in a dry garage or basement away from direct sunlight. An airing cupboard where there is gentle heat is also a good place. Dampness is the danger. When the material is quite dry, store it in an airy place where there is no likelihood of mice, birds or insects doing damage.

Helychrysum (straw flowers) should be picked just before they open, cut directly under the head and wired before drying, using a stub wire bent at one end to form a tiny hook and pulled through. Poppy seed heads and teazels should be allowed to dry on the plant, but pick reed mace (bulrushes) before they are fully mature.

Some flowers prefer to remain in water to dry off naturally, small peony heads, hydrangeas and pompon dahlias being examples. Long-stemmed roses, hung upside-down at the bud stage, dry to beautiful faded shades that are a joy to behold. Flexible stems, such as broom, willow and mulberry, can be shaped and tied, then left to dry into interesting shapes for special designs.

PRESERVING WITH GLYCERINE

Mature leaves, especially beech, do well in glycerine. Varied shades are achieved by treating plant materials for different periods of time and exposing the leaves to sunlight after preservation is complete. Pick undamaged deciduous sprays in late summer. Evergreen leaves can be treated at any time of the year and take on an attractive leathery appearance.

With woody stems, crush and scrape the ends and steep the bottom 2 inches in a solution of one part glycerine to two parts very hot water, topping up the mixture during the take-up period if the level drops. Adding a quarter of a teaspoon of chlorohexidine will prevent mold. Mix the solution thoroughly and leave the material in it for one to ten weeks depending on the leaf type; guidelines are given in the chart opposite. *Fatsia japonica*, fig and ivy leaves need to be immersed in a shallow tray and the leaves mopped over with the solution from time to time.

A cheaper alternative to glycerine is a half-and-half mixture of automobile anti-freeze solution and hot water, which gives a slightly different colour variation.

PRESERVING WITH DESICCANTS

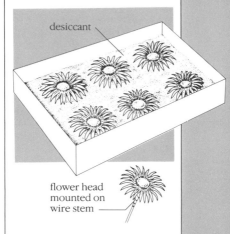

desiccant

flower head
mounted on
wire stem

Daisy-type flowers and orchids, which often give disappointing results when air dried, can be preserved in chemical drying agents such as borax or silica gel. Buy one of the commercial products if you wish to experiment and follow the instructions carefully. This type of desiccant can be reactivated in a cool oven. Sand can also be used; wash and rinse the grains several times and then dry on trays for four hours in a cool oven.

The desiccant method *(above)* consists of filling an air-tight plastic box with a layer of desiccant about ½ inch deep. Place the flower heads, with about 1 inch of stem attached, in the desiccant and gently sift it around until the petals are covered, keeping a natural flower shape. Replace the lid, seal the box with tape and put it aside for a few days. Test the

DRYING AND PRESERVING

flowers—they should feel crisp—and remove them as soon as they are ready, since overexposure to the crystals will spoil the petals. Store by pressing the stems into dry foam, without overcrowding. The flowers can be remounted on false wire stems and will give lasting pleasure. If your room is damp, the silica-dried material may wilt and need treating again at intervals.

PRESSING FOLIAGE

There are several ways of doing this. Ferns, bracken and bamboo, among others, can be pressed for winter use. Pick when the foliage is at its best and remove any damaged leaves. Autumn tints, which look so beautiful, indicate dying foliage, unfortunately, which will probably drop if pressed late in the season. Place the foliage between several layers of newspaper and slip it under a rug or carpet. Leave for a week or two, checking progress. Such dried foliage looks well with either dried or fresh flowers. Ferns look particularly opulent sprayed with gilt and used with autumn-tinted leaves.

An instant method of achieving the same effect is to iron the leaves. Pick foliage on a dry day and press firmly with a fairly hot iron on both sides, protecting your ironing board with thick paper or a cloth. Yellowing bracken, Virginia creeper or coloured leaf sprays can be ironed in this way to use in winter. Ironed foliage keeps its colour quite well but tends to be brittle to handle and lacks the graceful qualities of material treated with glycerine.

Simple flower presses can be bought from most department stores. They comprise several sheets of absorbent paper held together with wooden covers which can be screwed down tightly. Flowers and leaves can be pressed for use on greetings cards and in collages, sealed under glass or plastic film as a permanent memento.

SKELETONIZING LEAVES

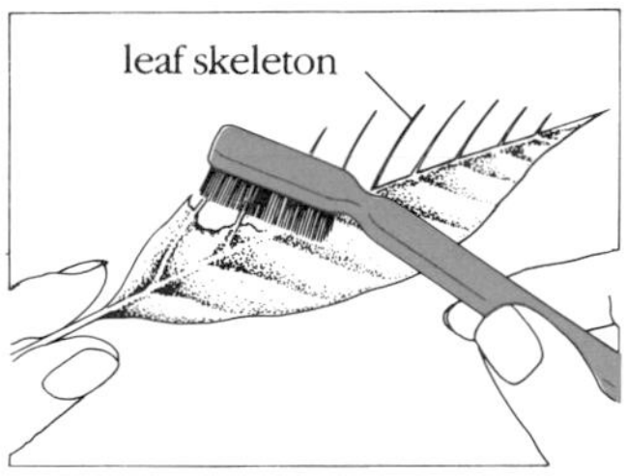

leaf skeleton

This is a tricky process, but such leaves bought from the florist are expensive so you may like to try it for yourself.

Boil 1 ounce of dissolved washing soda in about $5\frac{1}{2}$ cups of water, with 2 ounces of slaked quicklime. Boil the mixture for 15 minutes, then pour off the clear liquid and bring back to a boil. Add the leaves (magnolia works well) and boil for up to an hour if necessary, topping up to replace evaporated water. Test after 30 minutes: When the green pulp comes away easily from the skeleton, the leaves are ready. Remove all the pulp under gently running water; an old toothbrush is good for doing this (above). Dry the leaves off on newspaper and press them flat. Handle them carefully, since the skeleton is very delicate at this stage.

BLEACHING

Stripped willow twigs reveal attractive white wood when bleached. Some preserved materials can be bleached in the sun, but it is usually better to immerse them in dilute bleach solution. The results provide unusual components for a Japanese-style arrangement.

STORAGE

Dried materials should be stored in large plastic bags to which a drying agent, such as silica gel, has been added. Keep the bags in a dry dark place where there is no danger of damage from mice or birds. Florists' boxes are also useful for storing dried flowers and foliage between layers of tissue paper.

CRYSTALLIZED FLOWERS

Decorating a cake with real flowers which have been crystallized adds a delicate artistic touch. Any sweet-smelling flower is edible and keeps extremely well in a dry container. Violets, primroses, forget-me-nots and pansies are perfect. This is a reliable method for crystallizing flowers:

Mix together two parts of superfine sugar to one part of granulated sugar. Carefully add food colouring, if desired. Crush with a spoon and sieve to remove lumps. Next, mix 3 to 4 teaspoons of rosewater (from the drug store) with one teaspoon of gum arabic. Using a fine brush, carefully paint the petals of each flower with the solution. Then sprinkle both sides of the flower with the sugar mixture and leave it to dry out on waxed paper for a week. Store your crystallized flowers in a very dry cupboard in a pan punched with air holes to maintain a continuous circulation of air.

PRESERVING FOLIAGE USING GLYCERINE

ASPIDISTRA	12 weeks, mopping over often
BEECH	A few days, checking often
BOX	3 to 4 weeks
EUCALYPTUS	2 to 3 weeks
FATSIA JAPONICA	2 to 10 weeks. Submerge and mop over occasionally. May need stem support afterwards.
IVY	2 to 3 weeks. Submerge
LAUREL	3 to 4 weeks
MAGNOLIA	3 to 4 weeks
MAHONIA	3 to 6 weeks

Remove foliage from the solution when the colour is uniform, but before glycerine beads appear on the leaf surface.
Rose hips and some berries may be successfully treated with glycerine; when coated with clear varnish, they add a glossy variation to the matt texture of a dried arrangement.

*tree branch
display, p. 29*

*spray of
blossom,
p. 68*

DRYING AND PRESERVING

POTPOURRI

Small bowls of potpourri are wonderful for perfuming rooms or drawers; they can be revived periodically by adding a drop or two of essence. Here is a recipe for making your own mixture:

On a dry day, gather flowers, petals, leaves and herbs. You could collect, for example, scented rose petals, jasmine, buddleia, carnations, wallflowers, hyacinths and daffodils, and herbs such as rosemary, lavender, bay, thyme, mint and bergamot. Strip the petals from large flower heads, but leave small ones intact. Spread them out on box lids and leave in the hot sun to dry; bring them in at night and put out again the next day. As each type of petal dries out, put them in a plastic bag or air-tight container. Strip scented leaves into shreds and dry in the same way. An airing cupboard can be used but the results are not so good.

The next stage is to mix the dried petals with about 4 ounces of powdered orris root and spices such as $\frac{1}{2}$ ounce of ground cinnamon, $\frac{1}{2}$ ounce of ground cloves, $\frac{1}{2}$ teaspoon of grated nutmeg, the thinly pared rind of a lemon or orange, or a vanilla pod. The orris root powder is the preservative and the spices, which you can vary to suit yourself, give the musky scent.

To achieve a rose scent, mix together four handfuls of dried rose petals and one handful of dried mock orange petals. Add 2 ounces of ground coriander seeds, 2 ounces of powdered orris root and a dessertspoon of ground cinnamon, stirring them all together.

DRIFTWOOD

Sculptural pieces of preserved wood combined with fresh flowers make attractive arrangements, especially if you wish to add height and line. Dead branches hung with grey-green lichen are often used with artificial flowers for winter décor. Wisteria branches can be stripped and bound into loops before drying; when used with fresh flowers, they give a wonderful feeling of movement in the Japanese style *(above)*.

To prepare driftwood before bringing it into the house, soak it for several hours in a mild solution of disinfectant, then dry it thoroughly and remove any loose or decayed matter.

For a "stripped pine" effect, leave it overnight in a dilute solution of household bleach. To darken driftwood, rub it over with a rag moistened with wood stain or oil. Special treatments include the use of paint sprays or the metalic finish made for automobiles, particularly the gold one. The texture of the wood can be accentuated in this way.

Spring flowers arranged with moss and driftwood strike a natural woodland note. Fake snow and glitter lightly brushed over driftwood add a mid-winter sparkle to your Christmas festivities and, combined with sprays of berried holly and pine cones *(above)*, they give an inexpensive arrangement that will last well into the new year.

The beach is a good place to find sculptural pieces of driftwood, washed clean by the waves. They make an attractive foil for flowers. A branch of spring blossom or an exotic flower head shows off the texture of the wood to perfection.

How to Light Flowers

Direct lighting from front

Direct lighting from back

Direct lighting from below

Direct lighting from above

Direct lighting from the left

Oblique lighting from front left

Oblique lighting from front right

Top light with secondary light

Good lighting will show off any flower arrangement to maximum advantage. Consider the effective impact of flowers on the function and harmony of a room as the light changes from natural daylight to artificial light. The theatrical effect of low-voltage lighting significantly changes the drama of an arrangement: Spot lighting focuses attention on particular blooms, while uplighting throws interesting shadows and patterns across walls and ceilings. The diagram on p. 148 shows various lighting situations in action.

DAYLIGHT
The subtle play of natural light, filtering through lacy curtains or Venetian blinds, dramatizes a well-placed windowsill arrangement. Sunshine emphasizes the qualities of light and shade in the flowers. Famous artists such as Fantin-Latour, Van Gogh, Matisse and Georges Braque used light as an essential component of their compositions. By watching how the light changes in your room, you can learn where best to place flowers for maximum effect.

ARTIFICIAL LIGHT
The modern approach to flower design takes inspiration from the interior decorator's use of creative lighting. Experimenting with lighting is often overlooked when placing flowers in a room. Mirrors, for example, especially in dark corners, turn light back into a room. The image of flowers placed before a mirror is doubled, the real and reflected blooms giving an extra dimension to the floral design.

Artificial lighting falls into three categories: Directional, indirect and diffused. A comfortable room will have both functional and decorative lighting, with general diffused light and specially focused areas for work or displaying features of the décor.

DIRECTIONAL LIGHTING is concentrated in a beam. The light is strongly shaded to sharpen the illumination and thus highlights objects on which it is focused (hence the term "accent lighting"). The sharper the angle between light and wall, the harsher the detail. Lighting plant material directly in this way can produce a hard outline and is best used sparingly. Light beamed directly on flowers, particularly tungsten halogen spotlights, can also cause them to wilt. Such lighting throws objects into relief, emphasizes their texture, and produces strong shadows. The drama of twigs highly exaggerated on a wall can be a little unnerving and spoil the proportion of an arrangement. If you wish to use bare branches to create a special effect, experiment with spotlighting from different angles and distances, blurring the shadows. Check that the beam of light is not broken by passing traffic or in a position where it will cause glare.

daylight effects, p. 20, 22, 24, 78b, 97, 101

windowsill displays, pp. 90–91

mirror and uplighting, p. 25

double images, p. 31, 73t, 95

directional beam, p. 69, 96b

dramatic lighting effects, p. 21, 25

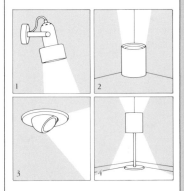

(1) SPOTLIGHT produces narrow concentrated beam, (2) UPLIGHT directs beam up and outward, (3) WALLWASH light is an angled form of downlight, (4) UP and DOWN LIGHT for special effects.

The fall of light on an arrangement is critical to the effect created, a fact well known to all the best flower artists. This arrangement of roses in full bloom was inspired by the work of Henri Fantin-Latour (1836–1904) who lit his flowers to perfection, and who studied each bloom as if it were a human face.

147

downlighting,
p. 22t

uplighting,
p. 25

colour effects
with
uplighting,
p. 23

HOW TO LIGHT FLOWERS

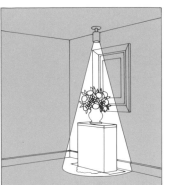

A downlight bathes flowers in a direct beam from above

A spotlight directed on a display casts a shadow behind

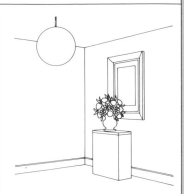

Diffused light from a ceiling fitting gives overall lighting

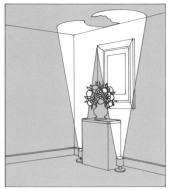

Two uplighters placed either side cast a tracery of fine shadows upward

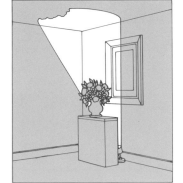

One uplighter behind casts a shadow and renders the flowers in silhouette

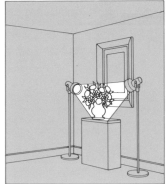

Two low-level sidelights create a pool of light against a dark background

DOWNLIGHTING is used to beam light directly on an arrangement from above, bathing it in a pool of light. The width of the beam can be varied: A narrow beam defines an area while a wider beam give more general overall lighting. A downlight over a dining table can be used to great effect to highlight a floral centerpiece. But do not have the light too close or leave it on too long since this will overheat the plant material.

UPLIGHTING an arrangement emphasizes the foliage and is especially attractive with exotic material. Individual flowers can easily be replaced when they wilt, enabling you to make the most of a few choice blooms with plenty of foliage. Directing light upward and outward creates the feeling of spaciousness. A sunlit effect can be suggested by floodlighting a white ceiling from below, with yellow or creamy flower arrangements to create a springlike atmosphere.

INDIRECT LIGHTING often provides more satisfactory enhancement of flower designs. By bouncing light off reflective surfaces, such as the ceiling and walls, pools of soft light are created, giving a room a cosy atmosphere.

DIFFUSED LIGHTING plays an important role in a room and is provided by chandeliers, translucent shades, standard lamps and ceiling fittings. Dimmer switches give the maximum variation of light from a single source. The total wattage of the lights controlled by one dimmer switch is limited, so check the amount of current needed when planning lighting schemes.

COLOUR
Most tungsten filament bulbs for general lighting give a "warm" effect, emphasizing the red-yellow part of the spectrum. They are more pleasing in the home than fluorescent tubes, which cast a "cold" light.

Under artificial light, flowers tend to lose their impact. Blue shades sometimes recede so far that the balance of an arrangement is spoiled. You can fit colour-coated bulbs or warm-coloured shades—or simply reduce the wattage—to achieve a warmer effect. Flexibility is important and a variety of lighting fixtures enables you to vary the accents at the touch of a switch.

CANDLELIGHT
The flickering light provided by candles is perfect with flowers and enhances glass and silver containers, masking tiny imperfections. It gives a "warm" cast and emphasizes yellows and reds. It also flatters people. But candlelight should be seen as a luxurious accessory, added only after the full lighting requirements have been met.

USING COLOUR

Flowers come in a galaxy of colours, with endless tonal variations and subtle blends. There is no better source of inspiration than to observe nature at work in the garden or countryside. The herbaceous border of summer flowers masses colour on a scale too expansive to mimic in an arrangement. But by studying the magical juxtaposition of colours, textures, form and scale of garden plants, you will expand your awareness.

By using colours as an artist would select them from his palette, and inspired by the works of such great painters as Cézanne, Picasso, Matisse, Dufy and le Douanier Rousseau, you can assemble flowers in a creative and individual way. Colour choice is a personal matter. Some people are instinctively attracted by bold primary colours while others prefer subtle tones and pastel groupings. Preferences can be influenced by fashion which briefly promotes unusual colours and combinations; as with many other aspects of life, colour choice may mellow with age.

HARMONY AND CONTRAST

While there are no hard and fast rules for colour selection in flower design, it is helpful to understand the theory of complementary and analogous colours, illustrated in the colour fans on pp. 16–17.

To see how colour works, look at the primary colours: Red, yellow and blue. They are pure and cannot be created by mixing other colours; but by combining the primaries, other colours are produced. Try it yourself with a box of paints.

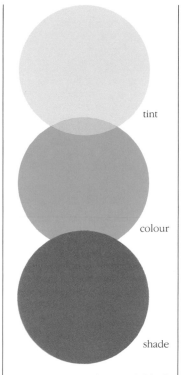

tint

colour

shade

A shade is a colour with black added to it; a tint is a colour with white added *(above)*. Related colour schemes can be either monochromatic, using various tones of the same colour (as pale blue to mid-primary to dark navy), or analogous, using harmonizing colours from adjacent sections of the colour fan (such as lime green, dark conifer green and turquoise). Since monochromatic and analogous schemes are based on close colour families, such schemes tend to range from "warm" to "cool."

Complementary colours, red and green for example, are opposites. By adding a splash of red to a foliage arrangement, the design immediately comes alive with a glow; imitate nature, with bright red berries set against glossy green holly leaves.

The colour of flowers has a unique quality, each flower ranging from light to dark, each petal varying in intensity. Some flowers, like anthuriums, reflect light with a clear hard brightness, whereas roses offer a velvety lushness of soft tonal colours. Study a single flower or leaf and discover its whole range of associated hues. The contrast of a flower with its own foliage is naturally pleasing, even if the petals are a hard brash colour that at first sight seem difficult to harmonize.

When choosing a blend of plant material or the container in which to put it, go back to nature and look at the way the colours harmonize within the plants themselves and with the surroundings.

Light not only gives flowers form and brings colours to life, but also shines through the petals. To capture light's changing quality is to discover the true magic of flower colour. Flowers set against a sunny window radiate their own brightness into a room.

Colour is never seen in isolation. The impact of a single bright yellow daffodil is quite different from the sunburst effect created by a mass of daffodils. For maximum impact, use flowers as solid colour statements, making a focal point in a room.

Choosing individual colour components is like fitting together a visual jigsaw, each part helping to build toward the complete picture. Link the colour of your flowers with the colour of your container and with the immediate environment—the table, soft furnishings, wall colour, art objects. The texture of surfaces also affects colour, as does lighting.

Finally, colour should be considered in relation to the effect you wish to create—a personal intimate atmosphere or a grand statement. Single specimen arrangements, scattered throughout a home, can be more enjoyable than a large bouquet created to celebrate a special occasion. The charm of the single flower placed with delicate effect is unmatched.

multicolour designs, p. 18b, 19, 28l, 88t

primary colours, p. 67

shades, p. 18tr

tints, pp. 114–115

mono-chromatic schemes, p. 43

analogous colours, p. 39

red and green arrange-ments, p. 21, 64l, 82l, 117

petal hues, p. 130

reflecting light, p. 21

velvety tones, p. 13

colour har-mony, p. 47, 78t

changing quality of light, p. 24

sunburst effect, p. 97, 106

colour state-ments, p. 101

single flowers, p. 89

USING COLOUR

*cooling effect
of green,
p. 88l*

*green
emphasizing
red, p. 75*

*variety of
greens,
p. 18tl, 78b*

*foliage dis-
play, p. 124*

*earthy tones
of brown,
p. 34b, 48, 129r*

*texture of
wood, p. 66l,
128*

*bamboo con-
tainers, p. 46*

*variety of
browns, p. 79*

*grey as a
sophisticated
neutral, p. 30,
124*

*silvery reflec-
tive surfaces,
p. 72, 73, 87b,
102tl*

*white con-
tainers, p. 35*

*setting the
mood with
white, p. 85,
95*

*clarity of pure
white,
p. 65*

*white-on-
white design,
p. 85, 125b*

*white as a
highlight,
p. 90t*

*gypsophila
sparkle, p. 72,
103t*

*balancing a
design, p. 74r*

NEUTRAL COLOURS

GREEN is the natural living background to the wide spectrum of flower colours. It goes with everything, since it is the "neutral" colour that flowers live with. In no other context would green be considered neutral.

Green cools other colours within a design, holds together a pastel arrangement and emphasizes the drama of a red or orange contrast scheme.

Although green usually plays a supporting role, an all-green foliage arrangement demonstrates beyond question the subtleties of tone on tone, texture and form. Appreciate the infinite varieties of the colour green in a mono-chromatic grouping—the polished emerald of the laurel leaf, the lime-green buds of spring, the blue-green of hostas, the silvery grey-green of the artichoke and the warm dark tones of branches and stems.

Foliage often lasts longer than flowers and, when it fades, it can be rearranged to look beautiful on its own. As an all-year-round colour, green brings the garden into your home, even in the depths of winter. Remember, too, that the green stalks are as important in a design scheme as the flowers themselves.

The absolute contrast to green is red; a red rose in a bush of bright green leaves throbs with vitality and demands attention.

BROWN is the colour of earth and wood, and the background to all the living colours of flowers and trees. It is mainly associated with autumn foliage and dried material. The rich browns of bark and wood can be highlighted by complementary flowers and containers. The strong line of a twig or stem lends emphasis to the design of an arrangement.

The brown of a polished mahogany table or a scrubbed pine dresser forms the linking background colour within the wider environment of a room. Whether your containers are pottery or earthenware, bottles, garden pots or special craft vases, brown is often the basic colour and provides a good homey neutral.

Brown has a multitude of shades, ranging from the pale colours of wheat, sand and grasses, through the warm earthy tones of wood and stones, to the darkest chocolate brown. As with green, a brown stem or branch has a natural vitality and richness of pattern, whether isolated or set within a group.

GREY is the third neutral colour in flower arranging. It may not spring to mind immediately as a colour, but what superb foliage is provided by plants such as *Stachys lanata*, *Cineraria maritima* and *Eucalyptus*. As brown can work as a homey shade, so grey is a lighter more sophisticated neutral.

In addition to the greys of foliage, bark, pebbles and stones, the colour range of grey is extended through to SILVER in the reflective surfaces of steel, pewter and silver itself. Crystal, mirror glass and chrome surfaces all have this reflective quality. The fashionable decorative schemes of the 1980s use grey equally well with soft pearly pastels or with rich bright primaries.

WHITE is a contemporary decorator colour which, in the context of flower design, encompasses white containers, tables, walls and countertops. Whether as a contrast, a neutral or mixed together with the whole spectrum of colours, white plays a unique role. It can express every mood, from the simplicity of a daisy chain to the magnificence of white flowers for a wedding arrangement.

Besides the clarity of the pure colour, whites are wondrously subtle in nature: tinges of green, yellow, pink and blue can be discovered in the first snowdrops, in spring blossoms and in the creamy white of orchids.

Examine white flowers carefully and note the other colours present. This will help you in choosing a container or foliage. If white flowers only are involved, a white container is the perfect choice. But since plain white containers are intensely eye-catching, they tend to detract from an arrangement of mixed colours.

Placing white flowers among other colours provides a highlight, as in a painting. Stand well back when creating such an arrangement and position your white flowers with care, so they do not draw too much attention away from the other blooms. Squinting through half-closed eyes often helps! A mist of gypsophila adds sparkle to a mixed arrangement, but larger white flowers may alter the balance of the whole design. Arranging large blooms low and to the center of a design will help the balance.

USING COLOUR

BRIGHT COLOURS

RED is bold, daring, exotic, brilliant, magnificent or romantic—a colour that quickens the heartbeat. Emphasize your mood by choosing red plant material with firm decision. Red roses express passion and excitement, but their soft velvety tones can be arranged to convey gentler romance. Anthuriums and heliconias, with their exotic polished impact, offer dramatic colour and outline. Shiny red berries linked with glossy foliage spell Christmas, while the red and white gingham of a tablecloth brings an informal charm that can be echoed in your choice of simple flowers and container.

Dispense with green leaves if you wish to emphasize the warmth of a design; clashing reds used for a special effect can be linked with dark red foliage such as copper beech or rhus. Make sure that the background does not lessen the impact.

Red is seldom chosen as a wall colour for the living room except by the very daring. However, since it is known to stimulate appetite and conversation, red is often used in restaurants and dining rooms. Red lighting (using coloured bulbs) flatters the skin but drains colours of their true value. This effect is particularly noticeable with blue flowers and green foliage.

Using red containers is tricky, because they can dominate the plant material, but ruby or cranberry glass vases or epergnes look attractive with casual flower groupings.

YELLOW, from pale primrose to deep golden, is a healthy, fun and joyous colour range, especially welcome during drab winter days. Yellow is a celebration colour, suggesting spring and sunshine; to sustain this feeling of lightness, keep arrangements of spring and daisylike flowers simple. Great bowls of daffodils make impressive colour statements. Sunflowers and lilies reflect the glories of summer. An abundance of golden leaves and harvest fruits convey the richness of autumn. Van Gogh's famous painting of sunflowers in an earthenware jug is one of the best-known flower arrangements; its timeless appeal captures the beauty and simplicity of the countryside in summer.

ORANGE is a hot striking colour, but not as dramatic as red and more difficult to use because of its "hardness" in a room. Marigolds and nasturtiums are examples of this colour at its most powerful. Orange flowers and berries are usually best reserved for autumn arrangements, but stunning effects can be obtained using orange fruits and flowers in brass or copper containers, with glycerined foliage or sharp lime-green leaves. Informal arrangements of orange flowers in earthenware containers are cheerful for a barbecue or Halloween party.

BLUE, merging into PURPLE, brings coolness into a room. Blue is a fresh colour seen at its best in wild flowers—drifts of bluebells or alpines, the sheer intensity of cornflowers, gentians and hyacinths. The very names of the flowers have come to describe the differing shades of the colour itself.

Blue and purple flowers suggest shadows and bring depth to mass designs. Used alone, blue can recede and is therefore difficult to use in a large display intended to be seen from a distance. However, placing a blue arrangement on a reflective surface helps to counterbalance this impression. Small bowls of anemones and alpine flowers are especially charming; a hall arrangement of tall delphiniums or irises, ranging from dark blue to purple, is magnificent.

Blue flowers against a yellow background bring to mind summer, vacations and the seaside. Arranged in a blue and white jug or in a pewter mug, blue flowers give a country impression, whereas the same flowers formally arranged in Art Deco glass impart a stylish atmosphere to a living room.

PASTELS

Mauves, pinks and creamy yellows create their own harmony. Mixed together they offer a soft ambience. Fresh green or grey foliage goes well with pastel flowers, as does the sharp lime green of spring leaves. Pewter, silver and coloured porcelain make sympathetic containers.

MIXED COLOURS

Assembling a bunch of flowers of mixed colours can result in fussy design. Decide what is going to be the focal point of your arrangement and then choose colours that tone and contrast. Bunching in the hand, then placing directly in the vase, is a useful technique here since mixed colours can be loosely gathered together in pleasing shades before placement (see p. 141). If a wide spectrum of colours is to be used, add plenty of green, especially a sharp lime shade such as that of *Alchemilla mollis*. Study some of the paintings by the Dutch Masters for the best use of a variety of flowers and fruits in mixed colours.

dramatic red,
p. 21

festive reds,
pp. 116–117

gingham as a
foil, p. 106

stimulating
the appetite,
p. 57, 119t

red contain-
ers, p. 121t

springtime
with yellow,
p. 101, 107

yellow fruits,
p. 48

autumnal
colours,
p. 128

dramatic
orange,
pp. 32–33

decorative
orange petals,
p. 57, 60

adding depth
with blue,
p. 18tr, 44

reflective sur-
faces with
blue, p. 31,
103b

pastel pinks,
p. 63

romantic
pastels, p. 47,
78t, 98, 114–115

sweet peas,
p. 87

mixed
colours, p. 18b,
19, 28l, 88t

FAVOURITE FLOWERS

The choice of flowers is as varied as personal taste. When selecting flowers, a combination of attributes must be considered, including colour, scent, foliage, life span, size and shape. Your choice depends on the type of arrangement you wish to create, the occasion, the setting and possibly your own confidence. Some personal favourites are listed below, arranged by colour for ease of reference, and with some of the outstanding features of each detailed.

WHITE

AMELANCHIER Snowy mespilus. Delicate sprays of white flowers in spring. Splendid autumn leaf colour.

ANAPHALIS Pearl everlasting. Good white dried flower with silvery foliage.

ANEMONE JAPONICA Windflower. Single and double heads. Also in pink.

ARTEMISIA Grey foliage for lightening and softening arrangements.

ASTRANTIA MAJOR Masterwort. Greenish-white flower heads, ideal foliage for mixed arrangements. Also a pink variety.

CHOISYA TERNATA Mexican orange. Fine heads of sweet-scented flowers. Shiny aromatic leaves.

CHRYSANTHEMUM MAXIMUM Shasta daisy. Long lasting and good for filling-in in mixed arrangements.

CIMICIFUGA RACEMOSA Black snakeroot. Creamy feathery plumes.

CONVALLARIA MAJALIS Lily-of-the-valley. Sweet-scented, bell-shaped flowers. Bright green leaves.

GALANTHUS NIVALIS Snowdrop. First flowers of spring. Perfect in a posy with ivy leaves.

GALTONIA CANDICANS Summer hyacinth. Single stem with many bell-shaped white flowers. Glaucous (pale grey-green) leaves.

GYPSOPHILA Baby's breath. Good with sweet peas and pastel flowers. Striking when used alone against a dark background.

HELLEBORUS NIGER The Christmas rose. Saucer-shaped flowers, golden anthers and dark green glossy leaves.

HYACINTHUS ORIENTALIS Common hyacinth. Beautiful waxy flowers with strong scent.

HYDRANGEA PANICULATA Creamy white flower heads in September, ageing to pink.

LEUCOJUM AESTIVUM Summer snowflake. White bell-shaped flowers, suitable for medium-sized arrangements.

LILIUM CANDIDUM Madonna lily. Majestic spires of pure white flowers with heavenly fragrance.

NICOTIANA AFFINIS Tobacco plant. White, also lime-green, flowers. Ideal for mixed summer and green arrangements.

PHILADELPHUS Mock orange. Long sprays of blossom, strongly scented.

VIBURNUM TINUS Excellent winter-flowering evergreen. Buds pinkish, opening to white.

ZANTEDESCHIA AETHIOPICA Arum lily. Unequaled for purity of form and sculptural quality. Marvelous massed or used as single blooms.

BLUE/MAUVE/PURPLE

ACANTHUS Bear's breeches. Beautiful leaves, white and purple flowers.

AGAPANTHUS African lily. Perfectly positioned flowers form an azure dome. Pale blue to dark blue to violet varieties.

ALLIUM Bright blue or purple flowers, often form perfect spheres.

ANCHUSA Intense blue flowers.

ASTER Many varieties, large and small flowers through a good range of purple, mauve and pink, including the Michaelmas daisy.

BUDDLEIA Butterfly bush. Arching branches with a profusion of flowers.

CAMPANULA LACTIFLORA Giant bellflower. Lavender-blue, bell-shaped blooms.

CEANOTHUS Shrub with flowers in various shades from powder to dark blue.

CENTAUREA CYANUS Cornflower. Vibrant colours, good for drying.

FAVOURITE FLOWERS

CHIONODOXA Glory of the snow. Starry blooms with white centers.

DELPHINIUM Stately showy spires of blue, purple and white.

DIGITALIS Foxglove. Graceful arching stems of large bell flowers.

ECHINOPS Globe thistle. Combination of blue globe flowers, silvery stems and dark green foliage.

FRITILLARIA MELEAGRIS Snakeshead lily. Pendant flowers with purple-checkered pattern.

GENTIANA Trumpet-shaped alpine flowers of an unmatched intense blue colour.

HYACINTHUS ORIENTALIS Common hyacinths. Strongly scented, statuesque blooms.

HYDRANGEA Lacy quality of "lacecap" varieties best for arrangements. Also good for drying as old flowers take on green hue.

LAVANDULA Lavender. Fragrant flowers that dry well.

LIATRIS Blazing stars or gayfeathers. Dense, thistle-like flowers on reddish-purple rods.

MUSCARI Grape hyacinths. Miniature, bright blue flower heads, resembling tiny bunches of grapes.

MYOSOTIS Forget-me-not. Beautifully detailed small sprays of blue flowers with yellow centers.

NIGELLA DAMASCENA Love-in-a-mist. Bright blue flowers; also varieties in mauve, purple, pink and white.

PHYSOSTEGIA Obedient plant. Spikes of mauve or pink flowers rather like snapdragons, with stems that stay in position when moved.

ROSMARINUS Rosemary. Blue or mauve flowers on spiky fragrant leaf sprays.

SCABIOSA Pincushion flower. Closely packed heads of lavender, dark purple or white flowers.

SYRINGA Lilac. Sprays of tiny flowers with the perfume of spring.

RED/PINK

ALTHAEA Hollyhock. Cottage-garden flowers for large arrangements. Single and double forms in a wide range of colours.

ANTHURIUM Exotic waxy blooms, valued for brilliance of colour from subtle pink to bright scarlet. Dark green, heart-shaped leaves.

ANTIRRHINUM Snapdragon. Lovely summer colours; red-flowered types with bronze leaves are excellent.

ASTILBE Feathery plumes of tiny flowers, with a cotton candy quality.

BERGENIA Early flowers that last well. Also evergreen leaves tinged with red in autumn. Last well in water.

BOUGAINVILLEA Profusion of brilliantly coloured papery bracts in reds, mauves and purples.

CAMELLIA Delicate, often short-lived flowers with strong shiny leaves.

CHAENOMELES Flowering quince. Waxy blossoms mature to quince fruits later in the year.

COSMOS Finely pinnate leaves with daisylike flowers, ranging from crimson, pale and dark pink to white.

COTONEASTER Bright red (or orange) berries borne in profusion in autumn.

DAHLIA Small pompon varieties, full of youth and vitality, are a personal choice.

DIANTHUS Pinks and carnations. Highly versatile and available all-year-round from florists.

DICENTRA SPECTABILIS Bleeding heart. Graceful sprays of pendant heart-shaped flowers combined with fern-like foliage.

EUPHORBIA PULCHERRIMA Poinsettia. Flame-coloured bracts are good at Christmas time.

GERBERA Excellent as cut blooms. Daisylike flowers in many colour varieties.

GODETIA Massed together, flowers look almost like giant carnations.

HAEMANTHUS Blood lily. Strange-looking, brushlike red flowers on snakelike stems.

HIPPEASTRUM Often sold under the name amaryllis. Magnificent flowers grown from bulbs.

LATHYRUS Sweet pea. Butterfly-like flowers in great variety of soft pastel shades. Wonderful scent.

LYCHNIS Campion. Bright purple or red flowers with grey foliage.

MONARDA Bee balm or horsemint. Strange shaggy flowers with aromatic leaves which can also be dried and used in tea.

FAVOURITE FLOWERS

PAEONIA Peony. Large lush flowers with strong attractive foliage.

PRUNUS Flowering cherry. Graceful branches of dense pink blossom.

PYRETHRUM Excellent daisylike flowers in a good range of colours from scarlet through pink to white. Available in double and single heads.

RIBES Flowering currant. Hanging bunches of tiny rose-red flowers.

ROSES A personal choice for summer perfume. Unmatchable.

WEIGELA Variegated leaves with pink trumpetlike flowers.

YELLOW/ORANGE

ACHILLEA Yarrow. Umbrellas of yellow flowers, good for drying.

ALSTROEMERIA Peruvian lily. Exotic trumpet flowers in rich yellow to orange-scarlet.

CALENDULA Marigold. Jolly summer flowers. Use petals to decorate salads.

CHIMONANTHUS Wintersweet. Waxy yellow flowers with crimson-purple centers, ideal for winter arrangements. Strong spicy scent.

CLEMATIS TANGUTICA Rich yellow, lantern-shaped flowers with silvery seed heads.

COREOPSIS Hardy, daisylike yellow flowers, with purple-reddish centers. Look well with grasses and seed heads.

CORNUS MAS Cornelian cherry. Clusters of yellow flowers on red branches.

CORYLUS AVELLANA 'CONTORTA' Corkscrew hazel. Strange twisted branches with yellow catkins. Produce strong outlines.

DORONICUM Leopard's bane. Yellow daisylike flowers, first to bloom after spring bulbs and valuable early in the year.

ERANTHIS HYEMALIS Winter aconite. Very early flowering; pick small delicate bunches for the table.

FORSYTHIA Good for forcing blooms indoors before buds open in the garden.

FRITILLARIA IMPERIALIS Crown imperial. Large impressive lily. Yellow and orange tulip-shaped flowers hanging in pendant clusters.

GAILLARDIA Blanket flower. Daisylike flowers, yellow and reddish-brown. Make long-lasting, simple arrangements in baskets and stoneware containers.

GERBERA Large daisylike flowers in unusual colour combinations.

HAMAMELIS Witch hazel. Early flowers, sweetly scented, and with spidery-looking petals, are borne on bare branches. Good foliage in autumn.

HELIANTHUS Sunflower. Huge daisylike head with brown-purple center on a tall stalk.

KERRIA JAPONICA Chrome yellow pompon flowers on long arching stems.

KNIPHOFIA Red hot poker. Spires of closely set tubular flowers.

MAHONIA Sprays of pale yellow blooms. Spiny leaves that colour well in autumn and blue-black bundles of berries.

NARCISSUS Daffodils and narcissi. The essence of spring, "good morning" flowers.

PHYSALIS Chinese lantern. Orange lanternlike calyx sprays that dry well. Good in baskets or earthenware.

RUDBECKIA Black-eyed Susan. Bright daisy-type flowers with black centers.

SISYRINCHIUM STRIATUM Creamy yellow starry flowers on slender stems.

SOLIDAGO Goldenrod. Plumes of bright yellow flowers.

STRELITZIA REGINAE Bird of paradise flower. An orange and blue flower with a unique sculptural form. Stands erect like a crest.

TROPAEOLUM MAJUS Nasturtium. Bright orange and yellow flowers.

GREEN

ALCHEMILLA MOLLIS Lady's mantle. Beautifully pleated leaves, cool yellow-green flowers.

AMARANTHUS CAUDATUS Love-lies-bleeding. Pale green tassellike flowers are borne by the variety "Viridis."

EUPHORBIA CHARACIAS Large greenish-yellow flowers with brown centers and grey-blue leaves.

GARRYA ELLIPTICA Winter-flowering grey-green catkins.

HELLEBORUS FOETIDUS Pale greenish-yellow bells with purple tips.

HYDRANGEA MACROPHYLLA Bracts turn greenish-pink or blue toward summer's end. Good for drying.

KNIPHOFIA TUBERGENII A greenish-cream variety of the torch lily, or red hot poker.

MOLUCCELLA LAEVIS Bells of Ireland. Tiny white flowers surrounded by pale green calyx. Long lasting and good for drying.

POLYGONATUM X HYBRIDUM Solomon's seal. Graceful arching stems with cream flowers tipped with green. Work well in all-green arrangements.

TELLIMA GRANDIFLORA Dainty pale green-yellow flowers. Useful pretty foliage of maplelike, bright green leaves.

Glossary

ACHROMATIC COLOURS The "colourless" colours — white, black, greys and silvery metallics — which are devoid of hue. In flower design, achromatics are used in containers as well as in flowers, twigs and foliage.

ADVANCING COLOURS The warm, long-wavelength colours of the spectrum — reds, oranges and yellows — which seem to bring surfaces closer to the eye.

ALABASTER A translucent material, usually white but sometimes streaked in red-brown, used for making vases. It is soft and easily marked, so needs handling with great care, but is a wonderful foil for flowers, particularly white blooms.

ANALOGOUS COLOURS Closely related colours which are neighbours on the colour wheel. Examples are yellow and yellow-green, green and blue-green.

BALANCE Stability achieved by even distribution of visual weight on either side of the vertical axis of an arrangement or a setting in which an arrangement is placed. In an arrangement, the actual weight of the plant material must also be "in balance" within the container so that it remains stable and does not tip.

BAROQUE A style of art developed in Europe and Latin America in the seventeenth and early eighteenth centuries. Central to the style are the themes of unity and balance, and works are often executed on a massive scale. Baroque flower paintings are typically exuberant and dramatically lit.

BOUQUET Flowers and foliage fastened together in a bunch. In French, the word is used to mean an arrangement.

BRACT A leaf-like or petal-like part of a plant or flower. The red "petals" of a poinsettia are in fact brightly coloured bracts.

BRIGHTNESS An ambiguous term, technically meaning highly saturated when describing a colour, but also used as a synonym for lightness.

BUNCHING A technique of flower arranging in which the flowers are first bunched in the hand, loosely tied with raffia or fine string if desired, then inserted into a container, lifted and gently shuffled into position.

CALYX The sepals of a flower that surround its petals. The calyx is usually a shade of green.

COLOUR The attribute of a visual sensation, or by extension an object or light, that can be named by such terms as red, yellow, blue and so on. Perceived colour has three basic dimensions: Hue, saturation and lightness.

COLOUR WHEEL A convenient circular depiction of the relationship between primary, secondary and tertiary colours, arranged clockwise in their spectral order. In the colour wheel, analogous colours border each other, while complementary colours are precisely opposite each other, making the colour wheel a useful reference for colour schemes.

COMPLEMENTARY COLOURS Pairs of colours which, when mixed together, produce grey: Red and green, blue and orange, yellow and purple, for instance. Complementary colours are directly opposite one another on the colour wheel and, in use, are dynamically contrasting.

COOL COLOURS Generally those in the shorter wavelength, green-to-blue-to-violet half of the spectrum, although yellow-greens and reddish-violets are considered "intermediate" in temperature. The colours with blue and green content have naturally cool associations with sky, water and foliage.

DOMINANCE Emphasis of one part of an arrangement over another, which may be brought about by the size of the material or its colour. An advancing colour will appear to dominate an arrangement.

DRIFTWOOD Sculptural form of natural wood used as an accessory or container for flowers. Found on the seashore or river bank.

FLORIST'S TUBE Small glass tube or vial in which fresh flowers such as orchids are sold. These tubes are useful for many types of flower designs.

FOAM A stiff but spongelike material used to support flowers in an arrangement. The cut flower stems are pressed into the foam, which holds them in place.

FOCAL POINT The point of an arrangement to which the eye is naturally drawn.

FORCING A technique of treating plants to hasten their flowering season. Bulbs that naturally flower in spring, for example, are "forced" to make them bloom in midwinter.

FORM The shape and structure of a whole arrangement, as distinct from its component parts.

GLAUCOUS A word used to describe a leaf or some other part of a plant that is whitish-green or grey-green in colour, often with a coating of powder, wax or fine hairs that can be rubbed off.

HUE The "colour of colour"; the attribute of colour by which it is distinguished from another. All colours are judged to be similar to one, or a proportion of two, of the spectral hues: Red, orange, yellow, green, blue, indigo and violet. Scarlet and pink, although different colours, are related by hue. Physically, hue is determined by wavelength.

IKEBANA Japanese style of flower arranging. As a rule, few blooms are used and the way in which they are used imparts a definite message, so giving the arrangement "meaning."

KENZAN Another name for a pinholder.

LIGHT Electromagnetic radiation capable of stimulating the eye to produce visual sensations. All colour is composed of light.

LIGHTNESS The dimension of a surface colour falling between white and black, through an intermediate series of greys. Also sometimes referred to as value — the amount of incident light a colour sample appears to reflect. The measure of how white or black, dark or light a colour appears.

LINE The shape of a design which is determined by the use of plant material and the choice of container.

MASS ARRANGEMENT An arrangement consisting of flowers or other plant material all of the same colour and type.

MECHANICS Term for the basic equipment, such as foam or other supports, used for keeping an arrangement in place. The mechanics of an arrangement are invisible in use unless they consist of natural materials such as twigs and branches.

MOBILE Plant material used to give the impression of floating in space, with all parts capable of movement.

MONOCHROMATIC Although literally it means containing only one colour, in flower-arranging terms it describes a scheme based around a single-colour family. Thus it might consist of sky-blue, Wedgwood blue and navy. The same monochromatic scheme could incorporate various achromatics, such as white, grey and silver, and still be termed monochromatic.

NEUTRAL A colour which does not clash or conflict with any other and which, therefore, may be incorporated into any scheme. In flower design, green and brown are considered neutral colours, although this is not true in other decorative contexts.

NOSEGAY A small bunch of sweetly smelling flowers. It can be made up in the form of a posy, surrounded by a frilly ruff; tussie mussie is an old-fashioned term for nosegay.

PASTELS The soft, white-added tints of a colour. When expressed as pastels, normally contrasting colours are reconciled.

PEDESTAL A stand for raising the level of a formal flower arrangement for display purposes.

PINHOLDER A metal device consisting of a base from which rise metal pins. In arrangements, stems are impaled on these pins or pushed between them. Also called a kenzan.

POT-ET-FLEUR An arrangement consisting of cut flowers and potted plants all within a single container.

PRIMARY COLOURS Red, blue and yellow. The three pure unmixed colours from which all others are derived and which cannot themselves be produced by any mixture. Green is considered a "psychological" primary, although it can be produced by mixing yellow and blue.

PROPORTION A pleasing harmony of shape and size in which colour, texture and form also play an important part.

RECEDING COLOURS The cool, shorter-wavelength colours, such as blue, green and violet, which appear to move away from the viewer, giving an impression of distance and space.

REEL WIRE Fine wire used by florists for wiring smaller flowers.

SATURATION The term used to describe the strength or vividness of a hue. Red, for example, can range in saturation from greyish-dove pink to a rich vermilion. High saturation indicates a pure colour, low saturation a greyed one.

SCALE The relative sizes of the individual parts of an arrangement; also the dimensional relationship between an arrangement and its setting.

SEAGLASS Pieces of glass found on the seashore which have been rubbed smooth by the action of the waves.

SEALING The technique of closing off the cut end of a stem. Usually this is done by dipping the stem end in boiling water or putting it into a flame. Flaming a stem end is also described as searing.

SECONDARY COLOURS Orange, green and purple — the colours resulting from an equal mixture of two primaries.

SHADE In common usage, a colour differing slightly from a specified hue or colour (for example a "shade of blue" or a "greyish-green shade"). Technically, shade is a term used to define degrees of lightness, indicating a pure colour that has been mixed with grey or black.

SPACE Openness that is an integral part of a design. Space is a quality widely used in the modern art of flower design.

STILL-LIFE An immobile grouping of plant material. It may also contain fruits and other "accessories."

STUB WIRES Cut wires sold in different weights and used for wiring floral work.

SWAG A collection of fresh or dried arrangements linked together for hanging. Similar to a garland.

TERTIARY COLOURS Colours lying between a primary and a secondary on the colour wheel. Or, intermediate colours resulting from a mixture of two secondary colours, the tones varying with the proportion of the mixture, such as russet or olive.

TINT A colour or pigment containing a large amount of white, referred to as a pastel. In common usage, a colour appearing weakly to modify another.

TONAL VALUE The gradations of one colour from light to dark. Pink is a light value (or tint) of red; maroon is a dark value (or shade).

TONE A synonym for lightness. Also a colour differing slightly in any way from a specified colour — as in "a tone of green". A colour that modifies another.

TROMPE-L'OEIL From the French, to "fool the eye" — decorative illusions, typically of a third dimension or imitative of costly materials or elaborate architectural detail.

TUSSIE MUSSIE Old-fashioned term for a nosegay.

WARM COLOURS Those colours in the long-wavelength, red-orange-yellow half of the colour wheel. Also known as advancing colours. They can make small arrangements look more imposing.

Index

A

Åalto, Alvar 66
adhesive tape 141
arrangements: "add-to-and-take-away" 35; altering size visually 62, 72; anchoring 49, 50, 64, 70, 98, 114, 138, 139; "architectural" 129; asymmetrical 49, 83, 84, 88; autumn 151; balancing 20, 73, 94; barbecue 151; black and white 83; blue and white 45; blue/purple 151; breakfast 108, 118; brown 150; buffet table 52, 118, 142; bureau 68; with candles 38, 41, 59, 148; candlesticks 112, 137; central 42; above central heating 74; centerpiece 52, 59, 113, 148; changing mood of 34, 147; changing form of 23, 49; for children 50; classical influences 8; cocktail cabinet 70; cocktails 120; coffee break 108; coordinating with container 136; "country" 28, 90; crescent 26; crownlike 50; dessert, 59; "disarranged" 98; disguising fixings 132, 140; dramatic 32; dried 32, 34, 122, 144; effect of colour on 151; effect of vase-life on 73; emphasizing shape 24; extending impact of 72; eye-level 92; festive table 119; "floating" 38; floor 26, 28; "flowering fruit" 38; as focal point 149; free form 22, 62, 72; fresh and dry 92, 132, 144; "garden" 36, 46, 72, 99; geometry of 42; as gifts 133; giving visual balance 45; graphic 100; green 59, 150; green and white 18, 94, 113; grey 124, 150; guest room 96; Halloween 151; with handkerchief 97; hanging 143; "headdress" 80, 103; "hedgerow" 49; improvised 38; individual 41; informal 42, 45; interplay of 74; intimate 74, 94, 106; jungle effect 104; "knot garden" 142; from leftovers 105; matching wallpaper 68; mechanics 139-40; miniature 26, 36, 62, 68, 142; minimal material 64; mirror image 102; mixed colour 151; mobile 34, 112; modular 42; multiple 69, 74; name card 112; natural 62, 69; "nests" 46, 61; "non-arranged" 82; off-balance 70; orange 151; oriental mood 9, 47, 49, 64, 92, 146; party table, 110, 120; pastel 46, 66, 113, 151; permanent dried 129; personalized 38; picnic 56;

pink/mauve 113; pink and yellow 78; placement of objects with 31; play of light on 24; with potted plants 36; proportions of 59, 76; pyramid 142; rainbow-coloured 88; red 151; red and green 82; red and yellow 88; refreshing 34; repeating themes 42, 62, 70, 76, 77; romantic 47; for salads 60; sculptural 20, 66, 96; securing 38, 42, 119; side table 59, 86; simple 70, 104; single stem 32, 41, 76, 88, 96, 141, 149; single colour 42; sink 103; spherical 66; spontaneous 78; spraying dried 144; spring 50, 138, 142, 146; still-life 47; supporting large 140; surreal 96; symmetrical 86; table 22, 23, 26, 31, 36, 62, 112; tall flowing 137; "thin" 84; topiary "trees" 31, 142; twisting 83; uninhibited 50; various levels 64; vase-life and 45, 49, 73, 98; Victorian 119; visually linked 45, 47, 50, 52, 56, 59, 62, 66, 74, 83, 88, 94, 108; wall 34, 35; white 64, 84, 90, 125, 150; winter 146; yellow/apricot 113, 151
Art Deco 100, 151
Auerbach, Frank 84

B

bamboo 46, 129, 135, 141, 145
bark 150; as disguise 132
bathrooms 94, 100ff
bedrooms 94ff
berries 41, 52, 142; effect of colour 151; plastic 132, 144
bird's nest 49
bleaching 145
bookcase 84
books as design element 89; ideas from 8, 14, 56, 59, 61
Botticelli 110
bouquets, individual 114
branches/twigs 49, 146, 150; arranging single 141; lighting 147; painted 23; securing 140; sprayed 110; stripped 28; supports for 28; as supports 90, 141, 142
Brandt, Bill 14
Breughel 8
buds 22, 41; single 94
bulbs, electric 23, 147, 151
bunching 66, 69, 78, 82, 87, 97, 99, 119, 141, 151
buttonholes 94; Christmas 118

C

cacti 79, 133
cake-decoration, adapting 142
candlecups 140
candles, anchoring 140; see also lighting
casserole dishes 106, 137

Cézanne 14, 149
Chagall 14, 132
Charlotte Sophia of Mecklenburg-Strelitz 32
chicken wire 133, 137, 139, 140, 142
Chinese style 10
Christmas 116–19
Cliff, Clarice 66, 97
cocktail sticks 38, 54, 138, 140
colour: artificial light 148; artificial material 132; bathroom 100, 102; bright 151; Christmas 118; choosing 50; complementary/analogous 149; containers 50, 136, 137, 138; contrasting 52, 79, 149; coordinated 66, 78, 124, 149; dried material 49; and effect 149; effect of light on 24; flowers 149-54; foliage 31; for hospitals 133; informal arrangements 45; juxtaposition of 149; linking 52, 56, 62, 110, 120, 121, 136, 137; living rooms 62; maximum impact 149; mixed 18, 28; neutral/rainbow 88, 150; office 122; pastel 36, 46, 113, 133, 137; primary 110, 133, 149; related schemes 149; repeating modules 41, 42; romantic tables 113; salads 60, 61; spray-on 120, 146; stem length and accent 41; using 149–50; using electric bulbs 23, 151; varying with seasons 90; weddings 143; when choosing flowers 132; see also arrangements
colour fans 16–17
cones, plastic 140
containers: alabaster 137; autumn 90; bamboo 46, 47, 49, 108; baskets 22, 28, 34, 35, 46, 56, 59, 66, 73, 99, 106, 120, 129, 138, 142; blue arrangements 151; bottles 32, 41, 50, 64, 97, 106, 118, 136; buckets 23, 26, 28; china/ceramic 14, 35, 56, 59, 73, 78, 79, 80, 90, 102, 104, 105, 108, 129, 136, 137; choosing 136–8; Christmas 117; clay 22, 31; cookie sheet 38–9; displaying food 59; dry displays 129; enameled 73, 106; enhancing 137; epergne 64; fruit and vegetables as 136, 138; glass 12, 23, 24, 28, 38, 41, 45, 46, 49, 50, 52, 60, 62, 64, 68, 69, 70, 72, 73, 74, 80, 87, 92, 94, 97, 98, 104, 108, 117, 118, 119, 136, 137, 138; handmade 92, 96; homemade 50; identical 87; individual 46; jelly molds 90; kitchenware 38, 49, 54,

90, 106, 108, 136, 137, 138, 142; marble 137; metal 79, 90, 94, 129, 136, 137, 138; miniature 41; "nests" 46, 61; office 122–5; orange arrangements 151; oriental 12, 129; painted 138; pairs 69, 70, 136; pastel arrangements 151; plastic 35, 50, 102, 138; pudding molds 38; red 151; roasting pan 21, 142; on shelves 84; silver 112, 137; silver, light and 148; single blooms 32; spherical 42; storing 138; trays 38, 54, 59, 99; unusual 56, 70, 82, 84, 136; waterproofing 36, 46, 137, 138; weighting 70, 76; white flowers 150; wiring for stability 34; wooden 138
cubes, glass 64, 87

D

Delaunay, Sonia 70
desiccating 144–5
dining rooms 36ff, 86, 110; lighting table 148
dirt, removal of 137
dishwashing liquid, on foliage 134
dressing rooms 94; bridal 120
driftwood 9, 126, 138, 140, 146
drinks, decorating 120
drying/preserving 144–6
Dufy, Raoul 12, 14, 149
Dürer, Albrecht 8

E

embroidery, inspiration from 14, 66
equipment 139–40

F

Fantin-Latour, Henri 12, 14, 72, 132, 147
feathers 34, 129
ferns 45, 104; care of 134, 135; dried 120; miniature 36; pressing 145
fireplaces 24, 73
fish with flowers 54
fixative, florist's 139
flower heads 38, 54, 59, 110, 112; dried 126; on food 106; individual 41, 88
flowers: alpine 151; blue 151, 152–3; boiling water treatment 134; buying 132; care of 134–5; central heating and 74; changing shape of 45; choosing 132; colour of 149–54; crystallized 144, 145; "culinary" 60; cultivated 50; cut-out 121; drying 144–6; effect of lighting on 148–9, 151; emphasizing qualities 24; favourite 152–4; food and 52ff; fruit and 47, 49, 54; green 154; hospital 133;

lighting 147–8; importance of shape/texture 42; for individual arrangements 41; language of 133; making the most of 130*ff*; mixing fresh and preserved 49, 126; nosegays 141; office 122*ff*; "painting with" 66; picking garden 132; red/pink 153–4; seasonal 62; souvenirs 62; new "species" 42, 59; topiary "trees" 142; transporting 133, 140; white 150, 152; yellow/orange 154
flowers, artificial 120, 126, 132, 143
flowers, dried and preserved 22, 26, 34, 38, 79, 89, 92, 122, 126*ff*, 131, 132, 143, 144–5
flowers, wild 22, 50, 132
foam, florist's 31, 34, 42, 49, 114, 139; for building structures 140, 142; for dried arrangements 138, 144; in garlands 142; in glass containers 137; for hanging baskets 138; soaking 139; vase-life in 133
foliage 26, 31, 59, 78, 150, 151; for accent 42; artificial 126; balancing effect of 45; care of 50, 134; central heating and 74; contrasting 104; dark red 151; evergreen 116, 119; exotic 73, 74, 77; with fruit/flowers 49; grey 31, 88, 96, 124, 150; ironing 145; lighting 148, 149; mass arrangement 31, 78; in metal containers 137; for nosegays 141; in office 122, 124; for pastel arrangements 151; from potted plants 119; preparing 134; pressing 145; treatment 134; water and 137
food 52*ff*; linking colour of 56; decorating with flowers 52, 106; on leaves 57; oriental 52; patterns in 56; presentation 52, 54
food cans as containers 138
fruit: in arrangements 38, 47, 49, 52, 54, 79, 90, 96; autumn 151; as containers 38, 136, 138; frosted 57, 144; with flowers 133

G
Gallé vase 68
garlands 114–15, 142–3
Gaugin 14
glass, for anchoring 132, 137, 140, 141
glasses 41, 88, 106, 136
glitter: on containers 138; on dried arrangements 144; on driftwood 146
grasses 22, 26, 28, 34, 50, 59, 78, 94, 99, 102, 104, 108, 129; air drying 144; as

camouflage 80; picking wild 132; dried 126, 132, 144; in metal containers 137

H
hallways 26*ff*, 79, 86, 118, 129, 151
herbs 60, 106, 108, 133, 146
Holman Hunt, William 47

I
ikebana 9, 141
"inspiration collection" 14

J
Japanese style 10, 64, 141, 145, 146

K
Keith Murray 129
kenzan *see* pinholder
kitchens 106*ff*

L
Lalique 74
leaves: as camouflage 80; decorative 52, 102, 112, 118; dried 126; edible 60; serving food on 57; preserved 132, 144; single 70, 77; skeletonizing 145; *see also* foliage
Lichtenstein, Roy 45
lighting, artificial 20*ff*, 147–8; to accentuate shape 69; with candles 38, 41, 59, 148; categories of 147; colour effects with 23; diffused 148; directional 147; downlighting 22, 148; effects of 16, 23, 24, 90, 147–8; floodlighting 148; indirect 148; low-voltage 23, 147; for multiple arrangements 69; office 122; red 151; reflections and 72; shelf displays 84; spot lighting 147; "theatrical" 20, 41; uplighting 23, 24, 129, 147, 148
lighting, natural 20, 22, 90; effect of changing 24, 90; maximum effect 24, 64, 147, 148
living rooms 62*ff*, 86

M
mantelpieces 84, 86, 118; festive 110, 116
marbles, for anchoring 98, 137
Matisse 12, 14, 66, 149
mirrors 24, 31, 62, 72, 73, 86, 94, 100; placing 147
Morris, William 68
moss 28, 36, 38, 42, 112, 118, 132, 133, 137, 139, 142
mold, preventing 144

N
nosegays 94, 119, 141
nuts in arrangements 38

O
offices 122*ff*
O'Keeffe, Georgia 79
optical illusion 26, 96
ornaments 84, 89

P
paintings: as design element 26, 45, 66, 74, 84, 88, 92; inspiration from 8, 12, 14, 47, 66, 72, 132, 149, 151
pastry decoration 59
pebbles/stones: for anchoring 50, 70, 87, 98, 102, 108, 132, 137, 139, 140, 141; collecting 140; colour range 150; as design element 9, 70, 79, 87, 99, 117, 126, 133, 136
perfume of flowers: in bathroom 104; as design element 69, 96; on dining table 36; on dried flowers 126; in sick room 99, 133
petals 16, 110, 146; to decorate food 52, 60, 133; dried 126; edible 60; *see also* potpourri
Picasso 14, 149; vase 80, 137
pinholders 137, 139; for arranging single items 141; for dried arrangements 144
plastic wrap 34, 142, 143
porcelain flowers 8
posies 26, 50, 84, 110, 112, 143; frills for 141
postcards as inspiration 86, 96
potted plants 73; in arrangements 36, 110; lighting 23; in office 122
potpourri 94, 133, 146
preserving solution 134; *see also* vase-life
Procktor, Patrick 88

R
raffia 42, 92, 140
reflections 24, 31, 62, 66, 72, 73, 87, 102, 103, 104, 147; colour range 150
ribbons 118, 143
Robbia, Luca della 8
Rossetti, Dante Gabriel 47, 99
Rouault 64
Rousseau, le Douanier 149
rubber bands 140, 141

S
Sackville-West, Vita 68
salad bowls 136, 138
salads 60
sand: for anchoring 70, 102, 133, 137, 140; desiccant 144
scarf decoration 97, 98
screen of flowers 62, 64
seashells: for anchoring 102; collecting 140; as containers 138; as design element 99, 117, 126, 133, 138
seed heads: air drying 144; dried 34, 126, 129, 132
shapes, contrasting 59, 79
shelving 84*ff*, 102, 103

sick rooms 57, 98, 133
silica gel 144
skeletonizing 145
skewers 54; for anchoring 138
slime, removal of 137
specimen vases 41, 76, 89, 136
spray-holders 143
staircases 26, 28, 84, 114, 143
stems 41, 125; emphasis of 76; long 26; for repeating modules 42; uniform 42; arranging single 32, 41, 76, 88, 96, 141, 149; as design element 41, 62, 66, 69, 70, 74, 125, 136, 150; preparing 50, 134; sealing 117, 134; trimming 119
string, gardener's 140
structures, building 142

T
table napkins 59, 118
tablecloths 120
tables: glass-topped 23, 72, 87; romantic outdoor 113; place settings 38, 41, 119
tapestry, inspiration from 66
texture: of containers 136, 137; contrasting 59, 79; lighting to emphasize 147; use in design 74; when choosing flowers 132
thorn stripper 140
topiary art 31, 142
Traeger, Tessa 14
trays 38, 54, 59, 99, 118, 136
tussie mussie *see* nosegays

V
Van Gogh 12, 14, 151
vase-life: effect on arrangements 45, 49, 73, 98; extending 64, 125, 134
vases 74, 80, 86, 90, 100, 129, 137, 151; pairs of 69, 86; wall 35, 94; *see also* containers
vegetables 54; as centerpiece 59; as containers 136, 138; as decoration 56, 90; salad 60
vials 46, 49, 112, 140, 142
visual links 45, 47, 50, 52, 56, 59, 62, 66, 74, 83, 88, 94, 108

W
wall bracket 34
washing soda, for skeletonizing 145
water 64, 76, 137; flower heads on 38; in Japanese design 72; keeping fresh 34, 35, 125; treatment with boiling 134; for transporting flowers 133
watermarks, removal of 137
weddings 110*ff*, 120, 143, 150
Whistler 47
windowsills 84, 90

Y
yogurt cartons 106, 140

Acknowledgments

The author wishes to express his special thanks to the
many kind and generous friends who have given boxloads
of exotic flowers and lent their apartments and homes,
vases and ornaments, for the photographic sessions.

David Austin, *Stunning Flowers*
Stephen Bailey
Diamond Bozas
British Crafts Centre
Crafts Council
Michael Dunn
Gered's of Piccadilly
Jenny Hamlyn
Paul Hutchins, *Wedgwood*
Erik Karlsen
Rosemary Ladlau
Patrick Morris
Beth and John Oldacre, *Sheffield Nurseries*
Robert Pollexfen
Jackie and Gerry Poulson
Clare, Nick, Mark and Paul Thomson
Michelle and Robin Townsend, *Avondale Park Nurseries*
Jacques Vellekoop
Victoria and Albert Museum Crafts Council Shop

PHOTOGRAPHIC CREDITS
b = bottom; *c* = center; *l* = left; *r* = right; *t* = top

The author and publishers gratefully acknowledge the
invaluable contribution made by Spike Powell who took all the
photographs in this book, with the exception of the following:

18*tl* Clive Corless; 18*tr* Clive Corless; 24 Clive Corless; 26 Bruce
Wolf; 28 Clive Corless; 30 Bruce Wolf; 38*tl* Clive Corless; 38*b*
Clive Corless; 41*tr* Clive Corless; 42*b* Clive Corless; 46 Steve
Lovi; 49*t* Bruce Wolf; 52–61 Bryce Attwell; 64*l* Clive Corless; 78*b*
Clive Corless; 86 Michael Dunn; 87*t* Steve Lovi; 87*b* Clive
Corless; 90*b* Bruce Wolf; 96*t* Steve Lovi; 98 Steve Lovi; 103*b*
Clive Corless; 104*tl* Clive Corless; 105*l* Clive Corless; 108*b* Clive
Corless; 116–19 Clive Corless; 120*t* Steve Lovi; 120*b* Clive
Corless; 121*t* Bruce Wolf; 121*b* Clive Corless; 122–24 Bruce
Wolf; 126 Bruce Wolf; 126–27 Steve Lovi; 129*l* Steve Lovi;
147*t* Peter Kibbles; 155 Steve Lovi.

The publishers would also like to thank the following:
25: glass urn from Mary Fox Linton; 37: tableware from *Coalport
China;* 38*tr* and 39: cutlery, plates, cookie sheet and pudding
mold "candle holders" all from *David Mellor*; 55: black bowl
from *David Mellor*; 56–7: glass from *The Cocktail Shop*, and
cutlery from *David Mellor*; 62–3: vase from *Homeworks*; 67:
pudding molds from *David Mellor*; 70: vase from *Homeworks*;
112*tl*: glasses from *The General Store*.

Illustrations by Hayward and Martin Limited, Kent
Index by Kathie Gill